STUDENTS'/TRAINEE

BUSINESS
administration
Level I

Carolyn Andrew
Elm Park College, Stanmore

Marian Clough
City & Guilds Verifier

Jean Davenport
formerly Tile Hill College, Coventry

Margaret Harradine
Elm Park College, Stanmore

Eileen Jackson
Hertford Regional College

Anna Kennedy
Tile Hill College, Coventry

Susan Smith
Greenhill College, Harrow

JOHN MURRAY
in association with
 **City and Guilds**

Business Administration NVQ Level I Students'/Trainees' Book
ISBN 0–7195–4845–4
Tutor's Resource Pack ISBN 0–7195–4847–0
Business Administration NVQ Level II Students'/Trainees' Book
ISBN 0–7195–4846–2
Tutor's Resource Pack ISBN 0–7195–4944–2

ACKNOWLEDGEMENTS

The authors and publishers are grateful to the following for permitting reproduction of copyright material:
British Rail for timetable p. 27 (Trainlines License No. TLB/91/3105)
London Regional Transport for London Underground map p. 27 (LRT Registered User No. 91/1439)
Federal Express Europe Inc. for mailing form p. 81

Diagram p. 90 by John Townson/Creation
Illustration p. 97 by David Anstey

© Carolyn Andrew, Marian Clough, Jean Davenport,
   Margaret Harradine, Eileen Jackson, Anna Kennedy,
   Susan Smith 1991

First published 1991 by
John Murray (Publishers) Ltd
50 Albemarle Street
London W1X 4BD

in association with
City and Guilds of London Institute
46 Britannia Street
London WC1X 9RG

British Library Cataloguing in Publication Data

   Business administration – level I:
   Students'/trainees' book.
      I. Andrew, Carolyn
      651.3068

      ISBN 0–7195–4845–4

Filmset by Wearside Tradespools, Fulwell, Sunderland
Printed in Great Britain by Thomson Litho Ltd,
East Kilbride

FOREWORD

City and Guilds of London Institute has a long history of providing assessments and certification to those who have undertaken education and training in a wide variety of technical subjects or occupational areas. Its business is essentially to provide an assurance that pre-determined standards have been met. That activity has grown in importance over the past few years as government and national bodies strive to create the right conditions for the steady growth of a skilled and flexible workforce.

Both teachers and learners need materials to support them as they work towards the attainment of qualifications, and City and Guilds is pleased to be working with a number of distinguished publishers towards meeting that need. It has been closely involved in planning, author selection and text appraisal, but the opinions expressed in the publications are those of the authors and not necessarily those of the Institute.

City and Guilds is fully committed to the projects listed below and is pleased to commend them to teaching staff, students and their advisers.

Carolyn Andrew *et al*, *Business Administration Level I* and *Business Administration Level II*, John Murray
David Minton, *Teaching Skills in Further & Adult Education*, Macmillan
Graham Morris & Leslie Reveler, *Retail Certificate Workbook* (Levels I and II), Macmillan
Peter Riley (Consultant Editor), *Computer-aided Engineering*, Macmillan
Tim Roberts, *Wine Appreciation*, Stanley Thornes
Barbara Wilson, *Information Technology: The Basics*, Macmillan
Caroline Wilkinson, *Information Technology in the Office*, Macmillan

BUSINESS ADMINISTRATION

City and Guilds Business Administration scheme (4400) was designed to accord with the standards of competence laid down by the Administrative Business and Commercial Training Group. Accredited as a National Vocational Qualification, Business Administration is assessed by means of ensuring that candidates are able to reach competence in the wide range of office skills in a workplace situation.

The aim of these *Business Administration* publications is to assist in the process of reaching that competence. The tasks have been designed to meet the standards of the scheme. In certain circumstances it may be possible to use the correctly completed assignments as part of the evidence that the student has reached the necessary standard, although obviously simulation cannot truly substitute for practice and assessment in the workplace.

CONTENTS

UNIT 1

FILING

ELEMENT 1.1 *File documents and open new files within an established filing system*

INTRODUCTION

What do you have to do?

▷ file documents and open new files within an established filing system

How well do you have to do it?

To achieve this you must be able to:

▷ classify (pre-sort) documents correctly for filing

▷ file all documents without delay in correct location and sequence

▷ store all materials safely and securely

▷ ask for help when necessary

What do you need to know?

▷ the importance of efficient storage of information

▷ filing and indexing systems (such as alphabetical, numerical)

▷ filing and indexing equipment (such as vertical, lateral)

▷ how to handle special or confidential files

▷ how to label new files and introduce them into the system

▷ where to seek help with unclassified documents

What do you need to be able to do?

▷ pre-sort (classify) documents for filing

▷ set up, sort and sequence card indexes, and cross-reference materials

▷ file documents quickly, neatly and correctly

▷ prepare new files and introduce them into an established system

▷ identify unclassified and unclearly classified documents and seek help where necessary

▷ plan and organise work within deadlines

BACKGROUND KNOWLEDGE

The type of classification in any filing system will depend upon the company for which you work and the type of information filed. Whichever system is used, documents are generally kept in chronological (date) order, with the most recent document on the top.

Alphabetical classification is used to arrange files by name, subject or geographical location.

Guide cards are used within filing cabinets to divide and identify groups of files. Primary guide cards are always placed to the left of the drawer. Secondary guide cards are used to subdivide the main areas and are generally placed to the right of the primary cards. Colour coding may also be used to improve identification of files.

Folders are always placed behind guide cards, ensuring labels are visible.

Miscellaneous files are provided for each letter of the alphabet and placed immediately behind the guide card for that letter. These folders will accommodate documents which do not yet have sufficient correspondence to merit a file of their own.

Alphabetical classification

Rules for alphabetical filing

1. Surname first, letter by letter (Able before Abraham).
2. Nothing before something (Brown before Brown Adam).
3. Hyphenated names treated as all one name.
4. Titles ignored (Capt., Dr, Sir).
5. Use of Mc, M' and Mac – all treated as Mac.
6. Foreign prefixes treated as part of name (De la Rue).
7. 'The' ignored in company names.
8. County/city/town name is important.
9. Department names listed first (Defence, Ministry of).
10. Use of St – all treated as Saint.
11. Numbers treated as if written in full (21 filed as Twenty-one).
12. Abbreviated names treated as if written in full (BBC filed as British Broadcasting Corporation, but cross-referenced as BBC).

Examples of alphabetical classification
Three examples of alphabetical classification are given below:

(a) By name

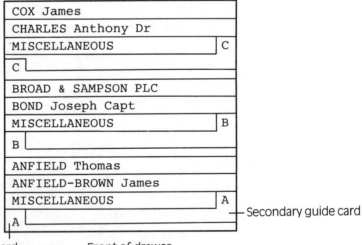

Primary guide card   Front of drawer

COX James
CHARLES Anthony Dr
MISCELLANEOUS   C
C
BROAD & SAMPSON PLC
BOND Joseph Capt
MISCELLANEOUS   B
B
ANFIELD Thomas
ANFIELD-BROWN James
MISCELLANEOUS   A
A

Secondary guide card

(b) By subject

		3 bedrooms
	Semi-detached	2 bedrooms
		3 bedrooms
	Detached	2 bedrooms
HOUSES		
		3 bedrooms
		2 bedrooms
		1 bedroom
FLATS		
		3 bedrooms
	Semi-detached	2 bedrooms
		4 bedrooms
		3 bedrooms
	Detached	2 bedrooms
BUNGALOWS		

Front of drawer

Primary guide card

Secondary guide card

(c) By geographical location

		Delange Pierre
		Armand Nicole
	Lyon	
		Le Moignon et Cie
		Distelle Sophie
	Marseille	
FRANCE		
		Kennedy & Harrison plc
		Bradley Harry Sir
	Yorkshire	
		Duffy & Clarke plc
		Bates K J
	Lancashire	
ENGLAND		

Front of drawer

Primary guide card

Secondary guide card

Numerical classification

Numerical classification requires each correspondent to be given a number, which is shown on the folder. The folders are filed in numerical order. New correspondents' folders are given the next number and placed behind the existing folders, as in the example below.

220

219

218

217

216

Numbers are then recorded against names on an alphabetical index:

Duffy & Co	310
Fairbrother P	216
Gates & Son	119

Cross-referencing

If a folder could be filed or requested under more than one name it will be necessary to decide where the folder is to be filed and put a note in the alternative place saying where it is filed. For example, Coventry & Warwickshire Hospital should be filed correctly under C for Coventry, but will need a cross-reference card under H:

```
for Hospital, Coventry & Warwickshire
see Coventry & Warwickshire Hospital
```

Some companies prefer to photocopy documents and make duplicate folders, but this requires extra space in cabinets.

Confidential files

The company will have a policy on how to deal with confidential and/or special files. This policy will generally include providing a secure area in which to keep the files, details on who is allowed access to them and for how long, and instructions on how long they are to be kept and their final disposal.

Old files

Company policy will determine the length of time files are to be kept in the current filing system. When files are removed from the system they are generally boxed and labelled and then stored in a dead file area to be retrieved as required. Some companies put all their old records on to microfilm or microfiche, which take up less space and allow easy retrieval.

Filing procedures

1 File daily – generally in the morning, before the post arrives.
2 Ensure documents for filing are 'signed off' by marking in the top right-hand corner, usually with supervisor's initials.
3 Pre-sort documents into piles; for instance, all 'A's together.
4 Arrange documents in date order with the most recent on top.
5 Remove paper-clips and staple pages of same document together.
6 File neatly – straighten all papers.
7 Apply classification rules.
8 Do not remove individual documents from the system – remove the whole folder if necessary.
9 Prepare 'out/absent' cards for absent files.
10 Keep a record of all folders contained in each drawer.
11 Remove old files and transfer to dead file area.
12 Open one drawer of a vertical filing cabinet at a time, to prevent it from tipping over.

THE TASKS

Resources required by students/trainees

▷ Task 6 – sixteen folders; a vertical filing cabinet
▷ Task 7 – office equipment magazines; glue and scissors

Filing

The list of files on p. 6 will be used to practise rearranging documents into alphabetical order by name, geographical and subject areas and also into numerical order. The key to the area numbers for geographical rearrangement and subject numbers is as follows:

Area numbers	Subject numbers
1 Cheshire	108 Screwdriver
2 Derbyshire	109 Power drill
3 Lancashire	110 File
4 Leicestershire	111 Bracket
5 Lincolnshire	112 Pliers
6 Merseyside	113 Drill bits
7 Warwickshire	114 Torch
8 West Midlands	115 Hammer
9 Worcestershire	116 Spirit level
10 Yorkshire	117 Tweezers

Using A4 sheets of lined paper to represent the drawer of a vertical filing cabinet, and the list of files provided, complete the following tasks. Ensure that you indicate which edge of the paper represents the front of the filing drawer.

TASK 1
Using either a typewriter or a wordprocessor, retype the list in alphabetical order by customers' names. Insert representations of primary guide cards for the letters of the alphabet.

TASK 2
Prepare cross-reference sheets for ICI, BBC, St John's Youth Club and 21 Club, and state briefly why, how and where you would use them.

TASK 3
Using either a typewriter or a wordprocessor, retype the list in numerical order by account number. If you have a sort program on your WP, obviously you will not need to re-key the list.
Provide primary guides at 1, 100, 200, 300.

TASK 4
Prepare an alphabetical index for the numerical listing of files.

TASK 5
Using either a typewriter or a wordprocessor, retype the list in geographical order using the area numbers provided to assist you. If you have a sort program on your WP, obviously it will not be necessary to re-key the list.
The primary guide cards are the counties (for instance, Yorkshire), and you should represent them in the appropriate place.

TASK 6
Prepare manila file folders for each customer, with the name at the top right-hand corner, and file behind the necessary guide cards in alphabetical order in a vertical filing cabinet.

List of files for Tasks 1–6

Customer name and address	Account number	Area number	Subject number
Taylor Transport Ltd The Square MELTON MOWBRAY Leics LE23 1NJ	197	4	108
Stevens & Hewins 51 Dickins Road GRANTHAM Lincs LI31 3BP	20	5	117
St John's Youth Club 91 Lawford Road LIVERPOOL Merseyside L16 1NU	301	6	113
R. J. Smith plc 10 Chapel Street COVENTRY West Midlands CV9 1TF	60	8	110
Capt. David Attwood 32 Langdale Drive WARRINGTON Cheshire WA2 5AZ	239	1	114
Robert de Measurer 19 Dartmouth Road WOLVERHAMPTON West Midlands WV4 5TA	28	8	112
Redditch Sheet Metal 13 Watling Street RUGBY Warwickshire RG2 9TD	108	7	108
Raymond J. McDonald 47 Forfield Road St HELENS Merseyside ST6 4NG	117	6	116
Dr Chandresh Patel 99 High Lane WIGAN Lancashire WI7 3JM	222	3	114
21 Club 7 Somerset Road LEEDS Yorkshire LS9 5FR	151	10	111
J. C. Hunt & Co. 135 Avon Road KIDDERMINSTER Worcs W30 5AT	165	9	108
MacDonagh & Sons 19 Commander Close WAKEFIELD Yorkshire WA7 4DR	375	10	117
R. Joyce-Carey Ltd 27 Brunel Close ASHBOURNE Derbyshire AH5 9TV	178	2	109
Alexander Dunne Ltd 13 Scotts Lane WIDNES Cheshire WA24 1TC	351	1	115
British Broadcasting Corporation Mill Lane LEEDS Yorkshire LS5 2JI	59	10	112
Imperial Chemical Industries Highfield Road RUNCORN Cheshire RU5 7AD	43	1	111

TASK 7

The following eighteen pieces of equipment might be used by a filing clerk. Mount a picture of each on the left-hand side of an A4 sheet and on the right-hand side give an example of how and for what purpose the equipment would be used.

envelope file
concertina file
card index box
rotary index
shredder
vertical filing cabinet
ring binder
box file
wheel index
tickler file
stapler
lateral filing cabinet
manila folder
lever arch file
vertical strip index
vertical card index
staple remover
heat binder

ELEMENT 1.2 *Identify and retrieve documents from within an established filing system*

INTRODUCTION

What do you have to do?

▷ identify and retrieve documents from within an established filing system

How well do you have to do it?

To achieve this you must be able to:

▷ locate and extract files and pass them on to the correct person

▷ keep up-to-date, accurate and legible records of all file movements

▷ notify promptly and explain politely any delays in the supply of files and documents

▷ ask for help when necessary

What do you need to know?

▷ the procedures for booking files in and out

▷ the procedures for tracing missing or overdue files

▷ how to bring files forward on a particular date

▷ the procedures for handling confidential and special files and the company retention policy

What do you need to be able to do?

▷ identify and interpret classification systems

▷ use filing and indexing equipment correctly

▷ extract files accurately and quickly from the system

▷ record file movements accurately

▷ carry out booking in/out procedures

▷ trace missing or overdue files and documents and request their return

▷ prioritise your work

BACKGROUND KNOWLEDGE

Booking out files

It is important to follow company procedures when removing files from the system. It is usual to ask the person borrowing the file to present an authorised requisition form.

A **file issued form** or **slip** will be completed by the person responsible for the file, after agreeing a date for its return. The file issued form will be filed chronologically by the **file return** date.

The folder is removed and replaced by an **absent card**, which will be updated each time a file is removed and kept as a permanent record of file movement.

When the folder is returned and the date noted on the absent card, the file issued form is completed and filed. Should the folder not be returned by the agreed date then action should be taken to retrieve it or to negotiate a new return date.

Bring forward

If future action is required on a particular document or file, it is usual to make a note on the document, such as 'bring forward on 12 March', and to make a note in a diary or tickler file to remind you to take the document out of the file on that date and present it for action.

A **tickler file** may be a card index box with cards containing primary labels for the months of the year and secondary labels from 1–31 for the days of the month, behind which notes can be placed to remind clerks to bring forward files on particular dates. The reason for bringing files forward may also be stated. Alternatively a photocopy of the document, with the bring forward date in the top left-hand corner, may be placed in an appropriate file (such as a concertina file) labelled with the months and days of the month.

Whichever type of tickler is used, it is important that it is checked each day and the relevant document(s) brought forward.

Tracing files

If the correct procedures have been followed it should be easy to trace any document. Generally, the filing system will be examined and the file retrieved.

If the file is not in position then the file absent card should be checked for information on who has booked it out and when it is due for return. A telephone call should be made to retrieve a file which is overdue. If there is no record on the file absent card, the file issued slips should be checked in case the information has not been transferred to the absent card.

If there is any difficulty at this stage in tracing the file, the file pending basket should be checked, and others in the office should be asked about the file. Sometimes files fall behind cabinets so it is important to check there.

If the company keeps a mail inwards book it might be possible to check who received the document in the first instance and trace back from there. However, if all else fails then the supervisor must be informed that the file is missing.

THE TASKS

Resources required by students/trainees

You will each require photocopies of the following:

▷ Task 1 – the file absent card and the file issued slip – one copy of each

You will also require:

▷ Task 1 – a folder

▷ Task 4 – a diary or card index box and supply of cards, or a concertina file

TASK 1

Complete the file absent card and the file issued slip from the file requisition slip provided. Prepare a file for the file issued slips and ensure all future slips are filed chronologically within it. Place the file absent card in the correct folder.

FILE REQUISITION SLIP

File name/number	Capt Attwood
File details	Letter 9 September
Required by	J R Jones
Authorised by	Tom Smith
Issue date	(today's)
Return date	(one week from today)

TASK 2

On checking through your 'files issued' folder the following week you notice that the letter to Captain David Attwood has not been returned. What action would you take to ensure its safe return?

TASK 3

You have been asked to find a letter dated 12 October from T. Hardcastle plc and take a photocopy of it to the Accounts Manager. On checking the file you cannot find the letter. Explain how you would attempt to trace it.

TASK 4

Your tutor has asked you to make a note on the letter dated 18 December in the R. Joyce-Carey Ltd file, for the attention of Judith Chewter, to bring it forward on 10 January. Do this, and then make a tickler file and enter the information necessary to enable you to remember to bring the letter forward for action on that date.

UNIT 2

COMMUNICATING INFORMATION

ELEMENT 2.1 *Process incoming and outgoing business telephone calls*

INTRODUCTION

What do you have to do?

▷ process incoming and outgoing business telephone calls

How well do you have to do it?

To achieve this you must be able to:

▷ answer calls promptly, politely and clearly in a manner approved by your organisation

▷ identify callers and find out their needs

▷ transfer calls to appropriate people

▷ find correct telephone numbers and make outgoing calls

▷ clearly convey the purpose of outgoing calls

▷ report faults promptly

▷ decide what information is not to be disclosed

What do you need to know?

▷ the type of equipment installed and what it is capable of doing

▷ how to use BT and other directories, systems and charge/cost of calls

▷ the structure of the organisation, its products and services

▷ the particular greeting style(s) used by the organisation

▷ the routine confirmation procedures used by your organisation

▷ the restrictions on information which may be disclosed

▷ the policy and procedures on security, safety and emergencies

What do you need to be able to do?

▷ use directories

▷ operate equipment efficiently

▷ report equipment failures/faults

▷ speak clearly and communicate effectively

▷ listen to and interpret information

▷ extract relevant information and compose messages

▷ take and transfer messages (written and oral)

▷ establish good relationships with colleagues and clients

▷ answer queries regarding your own area of work

▷ deal with wrong numbers and misdirected calls

▷ leave a message on an answering machine

▷ confirm calls by letter, memo, order etc.

BACKGROUND KNOWLEDGE

Using the telephone

When receiving a call

You should *always* answer the telephone promptly and clearly in the approved organisation manner, otherwise the caller may ring off thinking there is no one there. Get into the habit of holding the telephone in the hand you do not use for writing and *always* have a pad and pencil ready to write down the following information:

1 the name of the caller
2 who the message is for
3 who the message is from (firm/organisation)
4 the address
5 the telephone number
6 the message
7 the date and time

Always repeat the message to the caller to make sure you have written down the correct information. Ask for clarification of unusual words/spellings.

Never let the caller go before you have made a note of all the information you require.

Usually printed message forms are provided by your firm/organisation with spaces for the necessary information. If not, you must make sure that you have all the information you need as listed above.

When you have completed the message form correctly, sign your name as the receiver in the space provided. Once this is done, do not leave the message form on the desk or lying around; you *must* make sure that the message is passed on to the correct person/department as quickly as possible. Urgent messages should be clearly marked 'URGENT'.

If the caller wishes to speak to someone and you know that person is in the building, do try to locate him/her, *but* keep coming back to the caller to tell him/her what is happening. The same applies if an extension number is already engaged and the caller wishes to hold. You could say in both cases, 'I'm trying to connect you' or 'I'm still trying to connect you.' The caller knows that s/he has not been forgotten.

If the caller wishes to speak to a particular person who is not available, you could ask if the caller would like:

1 to speak to someone else
2 to be rung back
3 to ring later
4 to leave a message

Should *you* receive a call and then be disconnected, replace the receiver to allow the caller to dial your number again. It is the person who makes the call who should redial.

Sometimes people dial the wrong number either because they have fingered/touched a wrong digit or because they have not written down the correct number in the first place. If you receive a wrong number call, accept the caller's apology politely.

Remember, when you are using the telephone *always* be courteous and cheerful. Although the person at the other end cannot see you, s/he would like you to be as pleasant and polite as if meeting face to face. Try to keep a smile in your voice.

The telephonist is often the only member of an organisation that the public comes into contact with, so it is important that s/he gives a good impression of that organisation. A rude telephonist may discourage potential customers and create bad publicity, whereas a helpful person could promote good relationships, which are beneficial for business.

When you work for an organisation you may be the only person able to answer the specific queries which relate to your area of work. Remember to give the information clearly and concisely – callers do not want to waste time and money on the telephone – and also bear in mind that the caller may not understand the terminology and jargon which you tend to use with a colleague within the organisation.

Treat *all* business calls as confidential.

When making a call

Always make a habit of drafting the main points of your message before dialling, and have all relevant paperwork available.

Make sure you have the correct number before dialling. If you are not sure, check with your own list or the telephone directory.

Dial the number carefully, and if phoning another town and using a dialling code, give the equipment at the exchange time to connect you. Sometimes it is necessary to wait a few seconds after dialling before hearing the ringing or engaged tone.

Do remember when making a telephone call abroad that the ringing out tone and engaged tone may differ from this country; for instance, in Germany the ringing out tone is our engaged tone.

When the call is answered, tell the telephonist your firm's/organisation's name and ask for the person/department you require – preferably giving the extension number if you know it.

It is advisable to keep a permanent list of numbers required frequently by the telephone, or to use the memory on the phone itself for this.

The job of telephonist is sometimes combined with that of receptionist in a small firm/company.

THE TASKS

Resources required by students/trainees

You will each require photocopies of the following:

▷ Tasks 1, 3 and 6 – the message form – three copies in all

▷ Task 8 – the memo form – one copy

▷ Task 9 – the order form – one copy

You will also require:

▷ Task 1 – the pre-recorded message

▷ Task 7 – an organisation chart by the telephone with extension numbers

TASK 1

For this task, your tutor will arrange for you to receive a telephone call and you will need to write down the message.
  Obtain a message form from your tutor, complete this and arrange for Mr Barrowford to have it as quickly as possible.

TASK 2

The scrap of paper that follows was left on Mr B. Patel's desk while he was in a meeting. On his return he was very surprised. Why? What should the receiver of the call have done?

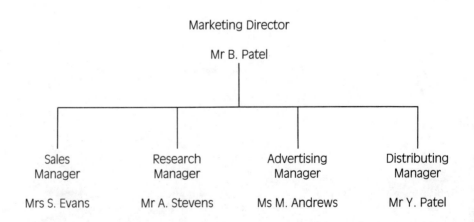

When discussing this with your tutor you may need to refer to the organisation chart that follows.

Marketing Director

Mr B. Patel

Sales Manager	Research Manager	Advertising Manager	Distributing Manager
Mrs S. Evans	Mr A. Stevens	Ms M. Andrews	Mr Y. Patel

TASK 3

Read the following information and complete a telephone message form.

The time is 1430 hours and you have just received the following telephone call from your boss, Mr Faruck Khan, from Mr Peter Baldwin of Catering Supplies, 120 Rochdale Road, Manchester, telephone no. 061–834 5168. Unfortunately they cannot supply the 200 dinner plates as promised. The manufacturers are on strike and he says they have only 150 in stock. The order could be made up with a different pattern from those ordered. Is this acceptable?

TASK 4

Mei Ling, the new receptionist/telephonist, arrives early one morning to find that the Reception area is under several centimetres of water. On looking round she notices that the water is coming from the ladies' toilets, though no taps have been left running.

Just as she realises she is the only one in the building, she sees Ms Childs, the Supervisor, getting out of her car. Mei Ling meets her at the door and asks what she should do. Ms Childs tells Mei Ling to telephone a plumber in the area and stress that the situation is urgent. She leaves Mei Ling to give all the relevant details to the plumber.

(a) Jot down the points Mei Ling will need to tell the plumber.

(b) Using the Yellow Pages, act out the situation with a partner. When you are satisfied, tape record your conversation on the available equipment.

(c) Play back and listen to your tape recording. Have you given all the details? Is the tone of your voice appropriate? Now ask your tutor or a fellow student/trainee for comments.

TASK 5

You could work in pairs on this task.

(a) There does not appear to be a list of emergency telephone numbers near the switchboard. Make out a list of those numbers that you feel would be helpful both to you and to other members of staff.

(b) You realise that it would be advisable to have a list of frequently used numbers. Decide what kind of a firm/organisation you work for and extract from the Yellow Pages names and numbers which you think would be useful.

(c) Both lists could be keyed into a computer. Try to arrange the lists in suitable order.

(d) Proof-read carefully before printing the lists out and placing them near the telephone.

TASK 6

You are the telephonist for Ace Travel Agency. You receive a telephone call from Mrs Alison Carter of 10 Mostyn Avenue, Salford, Manchester, telephone no. 061–736 5419.

Mrs Carter has just returned from a 14-day holiday in Greece and wishes to make a formal complaint. She never saw the tour representative during her stay and therefore could not complain or complete any appropriate documents there. Her luggage was lost in transit and was only delivered to the hotel five days after her arrival. The bedroom was immediately above the entertainment hall and the noise from the nightly disco kept her awake until the early hours of the morning. She did ask for a different bedroom but was told by the management that the hotel was fully booked. There were no excursions arranged despite their being advertised in the holiday brochure.

You say how sorry you are that she had such an awful holiday and promise to get the Manageress to ring Mrs Carter as soon as she returns from her visit to the bank.

Take the appropriate action.

TASK 7

You work for a paper manufacturing company and the following call comes through to the switchboard from the Goods Despatch Department:

'Get the fire brigade quickly; there's a fire in the large storeroom. Tell the Management and the Safety Officer at once.'

This is an emergency. What would you do?

TASK 8

You work as a Cost Clerk for Woodcharm Ltd of Gloucester, manufacturers of self-assembly furniture. They supply retail outlets in the UK and Europe, some of which are given below. The Cost Accountant, Mrs T. Reynolds, is responsible for calculating the sale price of the goods, which includes all overheads such as lighting, heating, telephone charges etc. To enable her to fix the selling prices she has asked you to compile a table of comparison of telephone charges based on a 5-minute call at various times of the day for the following places:

GLOUCESTER, HEREFORD, LONDON, DOUGLAS (Isle of Man), DENMARK, PORTUGAL, AUSTRIA.

Draw up a cost comparison chart and forward it to Mrs Reynolds in the form of a memo.

You will need to use the booklet 'Your Guide to Telephone Charges' from British Telecom.

TASK 9

You are employed by G. Banks & Sons. The Resources Supervisor comes into the office and asks you to phone the local stationery supplier to order ten reams of A4 bond paper suitable for the office copier. You need to find out the price and delivery time. Apparently the copier has developed a fault which has led to an excess number of spoilt sheets, so if stocks are not replenished by tomorrow, staff will be unable to use the copier.

Action to be taken:

(a) Look in the appropriate telephone directory for a stationery supplier.

(b) Prepare and make your telephone call.

(c) When you have all the relevant information, complete order form no. 5316 to confirm your action.

(d) Take a copy for the file.

TASK 10

Imagine you and your friends or family have read the advertisement that follows in the local paper and decide this would be the type of holiday you would all enjoy on the north-east coast. *You* are asked to make further enquiries.

SCARBOROUGH, Yorkshire

Modern holiday bungalow to let on beautiful site close to sea. Double-glazed; bathroom; fridge/freezer; central heating and colour TV. Sleeps 6.

Most dates available in July and August.

Ring (0723) 362483

Write down the main points to ask, such as the price, dates required, exact address/location, nearness to shops, railway station, buses, linen provided etc.

When you dial the telephone number given you are surprised that you are requested to leave your message on an answering machine.

Dictate your message clearly on to the machine. When you have done this, play back the message and be critical of your first effort. Re-dictate if necessary, making any amendments before asking your tutor to check the message for clarity and to confirm that you have covered all the essential points.

TASK 11

You will need to act out this simulation with another student/trainee.

A potential student phones the college office to enquire about classes, and the telephonist on duty tries to answer the questions raised. Bearing in mind the correct telephone manner, use the following information for your conversation.

Potential student	College telephonist
You want to know if there are any wordprocessing evening classes for beginners, and if so:	
which evening(s)	The classes are on Tuesday or Wednesday
the time of classes	from 7 p.m. to 9 p.m.
the length of the course	for 12 weeks – next course starts at the beginning of next month
which site	main site in Church Street, opposite the post office
the cost	£25
the possibility of taking an exam	exam at tutor's discretion, depending on the progress made

TASK 12

You are the telephonist/receptionist at the Barton branch of Focus Electronics. The Sales Manager has informed you that he is expecting a phone call from a very important customer.

At 9.10 a.m., a man approaches the reception desk. You have already checked through the Appointments Book and the first visitor should be Mr Gordon Seager at 10 a.m. The man is just producing his business card when the telephone rings. It is an outside call.

(a) What would you say to the visitor?

(b) What would you say on the phone?

(c) Which would you deal with first, and why?

INTRODUCTION

What do you have to do?

▷ receive and relay oral and written messages

How well do you have to do it?

To achieve this you must be able to:

▷ obtain and check all relevant information with the caller in a courteous manner

▷ pass on essential information, written or oral, accurately

▷ pass on the message to the appropriate person/location

What do you need to know?

▷ the structure of the organisation and location of the personnel

▷ the responsibilities of the personnel

▷ the correct procedure for passing on information

What do you need to be able to do?

▷ communicate effectively both in writing and orally

▷ create goodwill/good relationships with colleagues and clients

▷ identify the caller, the person/department the message is for, and how urgent the message is

▷ listen to and interpret the information

▷ take down the message from the caller

▷ ask for additional information or a repetition of the message if you are unsure of certain points

▷ check the message with the caller

▷ compose and write relevant and complete messages legibly, using correct tone, style, grammar and appropriate vocabulary

▷ arrange for messages to get to the appropriate person/department as quickly as possible

BACKGROUND KNOWLEDGE

When taking messages either:

- over the telephone
- from someone face to face, or
- in written form

it is important that you obtain all the relevant information and remain courteous at all times. You should listen or read carefully and write down in a notebook or pad exactly what the enquiry or message is. Do not be afraid to ask the caller or person to repeat the message if you have not fully understood or are not sure about the spelling of a name which could be spelt in different ways. It may be that you have interference on the telephone line and you cannot hear all the message clearly.

In any of these cases ask the caller to repeat the message, but remember to do so in a polite manner; for instance, 'I am sorry, I did not quite understand/hear what you said. Would you mind repeating that, please?'

Sometimes the caller may speak very quickly so it is important that you get the main points written down. It is advisable to keep all your notes, which should be dated so that you can refer back to them if necessary.

Whether you work in reception or on the switchboard – and you may have a job that combines both – you must always make a note of:

- the time and date of the call
- the caller's name
- the company's name (if applicable)
- the telephone number (and extension number if appropriate)
- the name of the person or department for whom the message is intended

Always verify the information you have taken down by reading the details of your written notes to the caller, and checking that you have the correct telephone number and spelling of the person's name.

Once you have replaced the receiver you need to look carefully at your notes and decide how you are going to write the message out. Many organisations have standard printed message forms which provide space for the date, the time the message was taken, the name of the person and/or department the message is intended for, the actual message you wish to convey, and the signature of the person who received the message. If there are any queries then the receiver of the message can be identified quickly and the problems resolved. The message form may have other details printed on it such as those in the example below.

Telephoned	
Called to see you	
Wants to see you	
Please ring	
Will call again	
Urgent	

Example of a message form

The receiver of the message will place a tick at the side of the appropriate instruction(s).

When you are satisfied with your written message and you are sure you have included all the necessary information, cross through your written notes to show that you have dealt with that particular task. The next step is to make the necessary arrangements to get the message to the person concerned as quickly as possible.

If you have to give a message over the telephone or to someone personally, do write the message out first to make sure you have not missed any important details.

Your messages are being read not only by your superiors but by many of your colleagues and friends; therefore if spelling is not your strong point do consult a dictionary. Try to use correct grammar and punctuation.

In a large organisation it is advisable to have a chart by the switchboard giving the personnel employed in each department and their telephone extension numbers.

THE TASKS

Resources required by students/trainees

You will each require photocopies of the following:

▷ the message form – ten copies in all

You will also require:

▷ Task 6 – cassette(s) with four pre-recorded messages

Taking messages

Do you always fully understand the messages that are passed on to you or do they sometimes leave you wondering?

The following messages were passed on as quickly as possible to the appropriate people, but do they convey all the details for someone to act upon?

Look at the original messages and you will probably agree that some necessary details are missing from the messages passed on to the people concerned.

TASK 1

Message passed on to appropriate person for action

> Telephone message received
> Mr Matthew Baron, Safety Officer
> Whilt you were out Star Safety Equipment
> rang. Telephone no. 061-726 7534.
> Suki Kaur

Original message

'Mr Khan speaking from Star Safety Equipment. Could I speak to the Safety Officer please? . . . Oh, I am sorry, I cannot phone back later when Mr Baron will be back in his office. Would you give him a message for me? We have just received the security cameras Mr Baron was interested in, and tell him these can be bought or rented. Perhaps he could leave a message for me if he is still interested. Telephone no. 061–726 7354.'

Now write out on a message form all the details that you think should have been included in the message.

TASK 2

Message received from Reception

> Miss Julia Broughton, Personnel Officer
> Two teachers called, to ask about some of us going on a
> telephone course. I think they were from the local college
> as I recognised one of them. I have looked in the telephone
> directory and the local college number is 92310
>   Zoe Booth

Original message

'Good morning. We are two members of staff from the local College of Further Education and would like to speak to someone about a short course we are intending to run on telephone technique. Have you a Personnel Officer? Oh, good, could we have a word with Miss Julia Broughton then please? . . . Oh, do you know if she'll still be off sick tomorrow? Would you please tell her we called? We are hoping to run a regular two-day course each month on the correct use of the telephone and wondered if you have any members of staff who might be interested in attending. Unfortunately the literature which gives full details of dates, time and cost is in the process of being printed, but we felt a personal visit to discuss the course would be appreciated. However, we hope Miss Broughton will soon be better and please ask her to give the Secretarial Section a ring if she is interested.'

Now write out on a message form all the details that you think should have been included in the message.

TASK 3

Telephone message received

Mr Robert Taylor, Production Manager
Mr Shaw phoned from the Estate Agents to say he has a house for you. Thinks it will be coming vacant soon. Telephone him.
                              Christine Jones.

Original message

'This is Mr Shaw from Billington Estate Agents. Could I speak to Mr Robert Taylor the Production Manager, please? . . . Oh dear! Well would you give him a message for me? Tell him I think I have found the ideal house for him – a four-bedroom detached which has been well maintained in a lovely rural area. I think he will be delighted with it. What's more, the people selling the house are moving to another part of the country just as Mr Taylor has done, so they want a quick sale. The figure quoted is in his price range, and I would advise him to view this property as soon as possible. Please ask Mr Taylor to telephone me immediately he returns from the meeting – he has my number. Thank you.'

Now write out on a message form all the details that you think should have been included in the message.

TASK 4

Telephone message received

Despatch Dept
Mrs Walker from 10 Riverside Road, Oldham, has just phoned to say her fridge/freezer has not been delivered. She is annoyed. Her phone number is 0706 86548.
Ian Parkinson

Original message

'Put me through to the Despatch Department. . . . Engaged? – I'm not surprised, probably someone complaining as I am! I can't stay on the telephone for ever, so will you give them a message? This is Mrs Walker from 10 Riverside Road, Oldham. Two weeks ago I ordered a fridge/freezer from you with special instructions that it would be delivered today, and I arranged to take a day's leave from work so that I would be at home to receive the appliance. It is now 4 p.m. and the fridge/freezer has not arrived. Can I expect it later? How late do the delivery men work? I have nowhere to put perishable foods as I have given my old fridge away. Had I not paid a deposit I would cancel my order. Tell the Despatch Department to telephone me to let me know what is happening. Stress that it is urgent. My number is 0706 86548.'

Now write out on a message form all the details that you think should have been included in the message.

TASK 5

Message received in Reception

> Miss Ruth Bailey, Office Supervisor
> Heather Richardson called from Burrows about demonstrating a
> word processor next Wednesday. Tel no. 0395 652752 ext. 321.
> Janine Finch

Original message

You are on Reception duty when a young lady, who has not got an appointment, approaches the desk and asks for Miss Ruth Bailey, the Office Supervisor. Unfortunately, Miss Bailey is on leave for the day. The visitor requests that you give her a message on her return to work tomorrow:

 'Say Ms Heather Richardson called from Burrows Ltd. We are demonstrating our new Burrows No. 6921 and No. 6925 Wordprocessors at our showroom in Linden Street, Sale, next Wednesday from 10.00 a.m. to 4.30 p.m. We would be pleased to see Miss Bailey and any other member of staff who is interested. If she cannot manage next Wednesday we could arrange another day when it would be more convenient for her or, alternatively, we could come here to demonstrate the machines when perhaps more members of staff could be present. Please ask her to ring me. Here is my card. My extension number is 321.'

Now write out on a message form all the details that you think should have been included in the message.

TASK 6

Ask your tutor for the cassette on which four messages have been recorded. Listen to them carefully. You may stop the tape or replay anything you have missed.

 Write down legibly the most important details from the first three messages on the message forms and make sure that they are taken to the appropriate person/department as quickly as possible.

 The fourth message would probably be better given verbally.

TASK 7

Your boss/tutor asks you to find out whether there is a normal train service in operation to London on Bank Holiday Monday; also whether a buffet car is available and whether it is possible to reserve seats.

 Telephone another student/trainee, who is acting as Railway Enquiry Clerk, to obtain the information, and then pass it on to your boss/tutor as quickly as possible.

 You will need a message form for this task.

TASK 8

Recruiting staff through a training centre
Role play the following:

- Mrs Kelly, Training Manager, Mayfair Training Centre
- Telephonist, Mayfair Training Centre
- Mr Bower, Martin & Culshaw, Solicitors.

Mrs Kelly will need a message form.

Telephonist: Mayfair Training Centre. Good morning, can I help you?

Mr Bower: This is Mr Bower speaking from Martin & Culshaw, Solicitors, in the High Street. Do you have a Training Manager?

Telephonist: Yes, it's Mrs Kelly.

Mr Bower: Could I speak to her, please?

Telephonist:	Yes, I'm trying to connect you.
	Hello, Mrs Kelly, I've got Mr Bower from Martin & Culshaw Solicitors on the line for you.
Mrs Kelly:	Put him through to me.
Telephonist:	You're through now, go ahead
Mr Bower:	Hello, Mrs Kelly, this is Mr Bower from Martin & Culshaw, the Solicitors in the High Street. I was wondering if you have any trainees who have almost completed their training who might be interested in the position of Clerk/ Typist/Receptionist at our office to start in about two weeks' time. We really need someone who can type at a reasonable speed and can use a wordprocessor. As you know, the Receptionist will be greeting clients, so we need someone who is pleasant, smart and courteous. Ideally we require someone who has followed an NCVQ Business Administration scheme, which is why I am phoning you.
Mrs Kelly:	What about the age of the trainee?
Mr Bower:	Perhaps someone between 17 and 22.
Mrs Kelly:	Well, would you like me to send three or four trainees for interview – at different times, of course?
Mr Bower:	Yes, that would be fine. Say next Friday, and make the first appointment for 9.30 a.m., following on at half-hourly intervals.
Mrs Kelly:	I will send you a letter giving the names of the trainees interested with the time of each interview, and I will ask each trainee to send a c.v. to you tomorrow.
Mr Bower:	That would be helpful. I look forward to meeting the candidates. Thank you for your help.

INTRODUCTION

What do you have to do?

▷ supply information for a specific purpose

How well do you have to do it?

To achieve this you must be able to:

▷ identify and access relevant information

▷ list and classify abstracted data

▷ supply correct information to appropriate person(s) within a required deadline

▷ report promptly and politely if there are difficulties in achieving targets

What do you need to know?

▷ how to use sources of information

▷ how to present information in suitable formats

What do you need to be able to do?

▷ interpret oral/written instructions

▷ obtain information and extract relevant data from a variety of sources

▷ plan and present information appropriately (such as notes and letters) and within required deadlines

▷ use dictionaries and other reference books/materials effectively

▷ check for and correct any error before passing information on to appropriate person(s)

▷ liaise effectively with colleagues and others

BACKGROUND KNOWLEDGE

We all need to look up information in a reference book at some time in our lives, and if we live in a city or big town the public library will have a large reference section which will contain books on every subject in which we may be interested.

The library at your college/training centre will also have reference books, adequate for the subjects you need to study, but probably the choice will not be as wide as that at the public library.

The Mail Room staff will be familiar with the *Post Office Guide*, and the majority of people will be used to locating and extracting information from the phone book, Yellow Pages, dictionary, thesaurus, railway and bus timetables, street directories/maps, and the RAC/AA handbooks. However, there are other important reference books which could be useful, such as:

Whitaker's Almanack, which gives general information on world affairs, statistical information on population etc.

Pears Cyclopaedia, which covers a wide range of topics, such as science, historical events, music, law, prominent people, general information etc.

Who's Who and *International Who's Who*, which give biographies of important and well-known people

Medical Directory, which gives information about doctors etc.

Not only do you need to know the reference books available, you also need to be able to locate and find the information quickly by making full use of the index and contents pages.

As information technology plays an important part in business administration today, you must be able to abstract appropriate details from information which has previously been fed into computers. For instance, a computer operator working for an estate agent can bring on to the screen specific properties to match the client's needs through the database files, such as a list of bungalows in a particular area and within the desired price range. This saves hours of searching through written records.

A viewdata system consists of a central computer which is connected to various adapted TV sets or microcomputers by telephone lines. The user dials the number of the central computer and can then look through a large amount of information by choosing to see the appropriate 'pages' or screens. Many travel agents use the viewdata system and can find out within seconds the holidays available to suit customers' specific requirements. It is possible to make a definite booking, and even pay by credit card by keying in the card number, as the central computer not only gives but receives information. This is obviously far quicker than the travel agent clerk telephoning various holiday companies, giving each one the specific details, waiting for replies, and booking.

Microfiche is the storage of information on plastic photographic sheets (known as microfilm if on reels). No doubt you have seen library assistants and bank clerks using these in their work. It is also used by companies who have limited filing space, as the documents are photographed and reproduced in minute form on a plastic sheet. When the information is required a microfiche 'reader' machine enlarges the document back to its original size. It is now possible to transfer information from a computer onto microfilm or microfiche without needing to print out a hard copy onto paper. This is referred to as COM (computer output on microfiche/microfilm).

THE TASKS

Resources required by students/trainees

You will each require photocopies of the following:

▷ Task 3 – the memo form – one copy

You will also require:

▷ Task 1 – your college/training centre letterhead paper (if available)

TASK 1

Imagine the names listed below are those of students/trainees at your college/training centre. You will notice that some have left the course before the end and have not returned the library books and locker keys as instructed. Draft a suitable letter asking them to return the items as quickly as possible – they are needed for new entrants.

Using the Thomson local directory, find suitable addresses for your area and be sure to use the correct postal codes.

Ms B. Ashton	left	locker keys
Mr S. Bellis	left	library books
Mr G. Bird		
Mr G. Bromilow		
Mr B. Hough		
Mr W. J. Jameson		
Miss S. Norris	left	library books
Miss K. Owen		
Mrs J. Patel		
Miss A. M. Ryle	left	locker keys and library books
Miss A. Settle		
Mrs B. Sheth	left	locker keys
Mr C. Thakkar		
Mr C. Westwood	left	library books and locker keys
Miss W. Wilson		
Miss C. H. Wong		

Discuss and confirm with your tutor the quickest way of producing these letters.

This task is required today. However, if you are unable to meet the deadline, inform your tutor, giving reasons.

Always check your spelling.

Either use your college/training centre letterhead stationery or simply wordprocess/type the name and address at the top of plain paper.

TASK 2

Four friends who live in the Manchester area have booked a holiday to Hawaii in May and the package holiday states that the flight must be from Heathrow airport on a Sunday. The plane leaves at 1810 hours and they are to be at the airport two hours before take-off time.

From the information given in the railway timetable opposite, select a suitable InterCity train, and check the London Underground map to find out how to get to Heathrow.

Make out a schedule giving the Intercity train departure time, its arrival at London Euston, and which lines/route they will have to use on the Underground. Explain your decisions to your tutor.

You must bear in mind the time factor.

Also, make a note of the British Rail Manchester telephone number in case any further information is required.

INTERCITY
Manchester and
Stockport → London

Sundays

	Manchester Piccadilly depart	Stockport depart	London Euston arrive
A	0110		0513
C	0110		0520
B	0110		0532
B	0640	0650	1019
A	0650	0620b	1019
C	0655	0705	1019
B	0840	0850	1222
D	0900	0910	1222
B	1045	1054	1417
D	1100	1110	1417
A	1128c	1148	1517
B	1238	1249	1622
C	1300	1310	1622
A	1300	1311	1622
B	1313	1322	1650
D	1330	1339	1650
B	1421	1430	1737
D	1430	1440	1737
	1610	1618	1909
	1700	1708	1955
	1750	1758	2034
	1800	1808	2053
D	1900	1908	2147
B	1900	1908	2154
	2013	2021	2316

Notes

A	Until 17 December	c	Change at Stockport
B	24 December to 25 March	fo	Fridays only
C	From 1 April	so	Saturdays only
D	Until 17 December and from 1 April	sx	Saturdays excepted
		mo	Mondays only
b	By special bus to Wilmslow	msx	Mondays and Saturdays excepted

Times in **bold** type indicate a direct service.
Times in light type indicate a connecting service.

For further information on train services, fares and other facilities, please telephone **Manchester 061–832 8353.**

InterCity train timetable

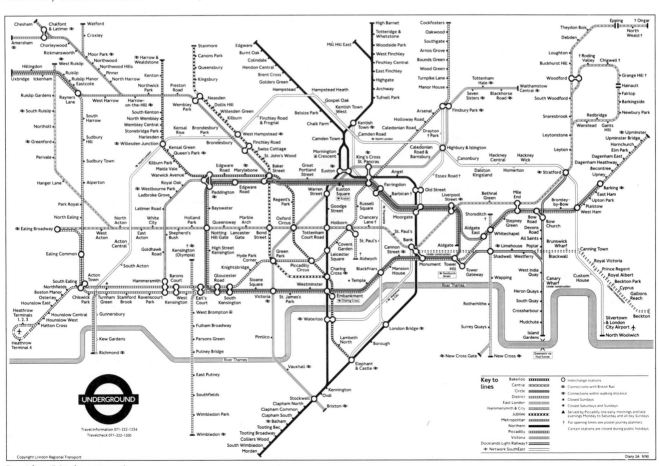

London Underground map

TASK 3

You work for an insurance company, and Ms Barbara Lewis from head office has just telephoned to inform you that they are opening a branch in Norwich. This means that your customers from the Norwich area will need to be transferred to the new branch.

If you have access to a computer, compile a list of all the customers in the Norwich area, and print out a list.

If you do not have access to a computer, either type your list or compile it by hand.

Whichever way you compile the list, it is recommended that you put the names in alphabetical order.

Then write a covering memo and send it with the list to head office today.

Customer no.	Name	Area
1001381	A. Edgar & Co	Norwich
1001433	C. Rawcliffe & Co	King's Lynn
1001365	T. Byrom	Norwich
1001403	P. Griffiths	Great Yarmouth
1001426	B. K. Quigley	Peterborough
1001422	A. MacIntosh	Norwich
1001395	M. O. Fernside Ltd	King's Lynn
1002360	Ackroyd & Co	Peterborough
1001451	K. C. Sandiford	King's Lynn
1001521	R. H. Taylor	Norwich
1001539	G. I. Webster	Peterborough
1001437	G. & O. Rishton (Insurers)	Great Yarmouth
1001389	R. R. Elderkin	King's Lynn
1001370	H. Calderbank	Great Yarmouth
1001418	J. H. Jackson	Norwich
1001363	J. Brown Ltd	King's Lynn
1001429	W. M. Ratcliffe Ltd	Norwich
1001394	Ferguson Bros	Peterborough
1001522	R. J. Taylor	Norwich
1001456	C. Saville & Sons	Great Yarmouth
1001485	R. Simm	King's Lynn
1001537	E. Waters (Insurers) Ltd	Norwich
1001401	S. Glover	King's Lynn
1001419	J. W. Jackson & Co	Norwich
1001445	D. A. Russell	Peterborough
1001464	W. M. Sharp	Norwich
1001499	A. Talbot & Co	King's Lynn
1001535	H. Waterhouse Ltd	Great Yarmouth
1001473	S. R. Shorrock	Peterborough
1001449	R. & M. Sanderson	Norwich
1001373	T. E. Cowell Ltd	Peterborough
1001435	B. D. Richardson	Norwich
1001410	A. D. Hillman	Peterborough
1001383	T. Edwards	Norwich
1001452	M. G. Santus	Peterborough
1001466	N. B. Shaw (Insurers) Ltd	Norwich
1001387	M. Egerton & Sons	Great Yarmouth
1001366	H. Byron	Norwich
1001372	W. M. Caldwell	Great Yarmouth
1001461	S. Shackleton	Norwich
1001516	F. H. Tattersall	Peterborough
1001397	A. B. Fielding	Great Yarmouth
1001424	G. & L. McIntyre	Norwich
1001440	E. L. Robinson	King's Lynn
1001376	C. Deacon (Insurers) Ltd	Great Yarmouth
1001470	D. & M. Shepherd	Peterborough
1001491	M. M. Smith	Great Yarmouth
1001412	Hirst Bros	Norwich
1001404	F. Grundy	King's Lynn
1001377	I. W. Douglas	Peterborough

TASK 4

Several disabled students/trainees from a centre in Northampton are travelling to Blackpool for a holiday in the minibus which has been donated by a local charity organisation.

Two members of staff – Mr Tony Summerfield and Miss Valerie Weller – will share the driving. The quickest way to get to their destination will be by motorway. In order to help the drivers, list the motorways to be used, and as the students/trainees will need to stop at service stations from time to time it would be a good idea to list these also. The starting point will be (M1) Junction 16. Set the list out neatly and clearly as follows:

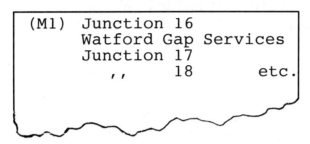

```
(M1)   Junction 16
       Watford Gap Services
       Junction 17
        ,,      18         etc.
```

It would be appreciated if you could give this list to the drivers by tomorrow as the staff wish to finalise all details by the weekend.

INTRODUCTION

What do you have to do?

▷ draft routine business communications

How well do you have to do it?

To achieve this you must be able to draft/compose letters and memos which must:

▷ be legible

▷ follow an approved layout

▷ contain all the essential information

▷ meet specified deadlines

What do you need to know?

▷ the general rules and construction for writing letters and memos

▷ the styles/layouts and rules desired by the people signing the letters for the firm/organisation

▷ the importance of the context in which letters are written

▷ the needs of the recipient (receiver)

▷ sources of information

▷ business English, grammar and vocabulary

▷ correct spelling and punctuation

What do you need to be able to do?

▷ plan and select presentation styles

▷ punctuate and compose grammatically correct sentences with appropriate language and tone

▷ compose letters and memos containing text and numerical information – for instance, enquiry, confirmation

▷ use a dictionary and other reference books

▷ access information from various sources

BACKGROUND KNOWLEDGE

The letters we write to our friends and relatives are called personal or private letters. The letters we write to firms/organisations are known as business letters. All business letters have a purpose – they may be seeking or giving advice, requesting action or making a complaint – and all play a vital role in running any business.

Writing is an activity which requires the use of various skills; business correspondence is a skill, and like any skill, it improves only with practice. You must write clearly and to the point to convey exactly what you want the recipient (receiver) to know and to do. Try to be courteous and considerate, and write naturally and sincerely. When you receive a letter which is rather rude, do not be tempted to reply in the same tone. Impressions are formed from the tone of the letter, and good tone in correspondence helps to foster good working relationships. As with oral communication it is essential to put your ideas into logical order to help convey the message clearly. Remember that when your letter is sitting on someone's desk in an office, it is that piece of paper which represents the firm/organisation you are working for, or even represents yourself if, for instance, you are applying for a job. The prospective employer only has that piece of evidence to judge whether or not you are suitable for the position you have applied for, and from the tone of the letter s/he may form the opinion that you would or would not easily fit in with those already working there. S/he cannot see you – that letter is your ambassador.

One of the most important features of a business letter is the way it is laid out. The firm/organisation will have special good quality letterhead paper which will show the name, address, telephone number, fax and/or telex codes, and maybe the names of the directors/executives. The following is a general example of a fully blocked letter with open punctuation.

TYGIL PRODUCTS
High Street
Chesterby   CT9 3MT
Tel (0206)56289
Fax (0206)15612

Our ref GB/JM

Your ref

[Insert date]

Mr R Mathers
General Manager
Palace Wholesale Co
Green Lane
HULL
HU3 4DL

Dear Sir [Salutation]

Vacancy No 14 — Senior Sales Clerk [Subject heading]

We have recently advertised for a Senior Sales Clerk and among the many applications we have received is one from Miss Dawn Thornton who is moving to this area and has given your name as a referee. Miss Thornton states that she has had four years' experience in the Sales Office of your company and prior to that two years' as a Clerk in the General Office.

We should be grateful if you would state whether you think Miss Thornton would be suitable for the position advertised — a copy of the advertisement is enclosed.

An early reply would be appreciated and will, of course, be treated in the strictest confidence.

Yours faithfully [Complimentary close]

G BOWERS
Personnel Officer

Enc
[This indicates that there is an enclosure.]

[Fully blocked means every line begins at the left-hand margin. Open punctuation means no punctuation in the date, name and address of recipient or after *Dear Sir(s)* and *Yours faithfully*.]

[The salutation *Dear Sir(s)* or *Madam* usually requires the complimentary close Yours faithfully. The salutation *Dear Mr/Mrs/Miss/Ms* usually requires the complimentary close *Yours sincerely*.]

A memorandum, usually referred to as a memo, is normally written to a person in one's own firm/organisation but not necessarily in the same building. It does not need an inside address, a salutation or a complimentary close. The tone of a memo is usually influenced by the position of the writer relative to that of the receiver. For example, a memo sent to the Managing Director would be more formal than one sent to a colleague in another section.

Sometimes memos are initialled or signed by the sender, as in the example that follows.

```
MEMORANDUM

To    All Staff                    Ref   JB/CA
From  Personnel Officer            Date  24 May 199—

Staff Development — Database and Spreadsheet course

Will staff interested in the above course, which will
be held on Tuesdays 9.00—10.30 a.m. for four weeks,
please let me know by the end of this month.
```

Memos can be sent by electronic mail.

Whether you send a business letter (to an outside firm/organisation) or a memo (internally) you should always take a copy of the document. This is one advantage that written communications have over telephone calls – you have a proper record of them.

THE TASKS

Resources required by students/trainees

You will each require photocopies of the following:

▷ Tasks 2, 4, 6 and 7 – the memo form – four copies in all

You will also require:

▷ Tasks 1, 3 and 5 – your college/training centre letterhead paper (if available) and envelopes

TASK 1

As Secretary of the Students'/Trainees' Union at your establishment, you have had a request for a representative from the local Citizens Advice Bureau (CAB) to come along to speak to the members about the general work of the Bureau and the help and advice given to the general public. The only time convenient for the talk would be after 3 p.m. on a Wednesday or Thursday. CAB is heavily committed at the present time, and you should ask for convenient dates in about two months' time.

Write a suitable letter giving all the details you feel are necessary. Address an envelope.

TASK 2

You are the Sales Manager's typist and you find the following note on your desk when you return from your morning coffee break.

Send a memo to all our Sales reps.
Tell them there will be an important meeting in my office on the last day of this month to discuss the reallocation of sales territory brought about by increasing sales and anticipated expansion.

9 o'clock start.

Give the memo a heading.

I will initial the memos on my return to the office this afternoon.

G. Turner

Note from the Sales Manager

TASK 3

Write the letter requested in the following note from your tutor.

Ms Janice Bolton, the NVQ Verifier for our scheme, rang this afternoon to arrange a visit for Wednesday of next week. Unfortunately I was out of the building at the time and had my diary with me.

Please write to her confirming that Wednesday of next week would be convenient. Suggest 10 a.m. arrival. She will be able to see some candidates being assessed on Unit 4 Petty Cash and on Unit 15 Reception.

Her address is:

'Dalegarth'
6 St Vincent's Close
PRESTON
PR6 2JF

PS Tell her I will arrange for a car parking space to be available and will notify the car park attendant to this effect.

This letter must be signed, placed in an envelope and in the Mail Room by 4.30 p.m. today.

TASK 4

It has been brought to the notice of the Health and Safety Officer in your workplace that some members of the staff have not been following the Health and Safety rules laid down by the company. For instance, the fire doors have been left open on many occasions; fire exits are being blocked; employees are smoking in forbidden areas; and during a recent cold spell the portable electric fires have been moved from their recognised position to nearer the employees' feet, causing the flex to be stretched across the office, and one member of staff has tripped over the flex. Fortunately she was not seriously hurt.

As you work for the Health and Safety Officer, Mrs Janet Arkwright, she has asked you to draft a memo to all members of staff as soon as possible reminding them of the need to adhere to the Health and Safety rules at all times. It is the duty of *all* members of staff to help prevent accidents!

TASK 5

Your college/training centre has decided to have vertical blinds fitted to the windows in the room where you have your communications tuition.

Find the names and addresses of three local suppliers and write a suitable letter asking for literature, samples and price lists. You will need to:

- state the window measurements
- ask how long it would take to have the blinds fitted after placing an order
- ask if there are any special terms or discounts available
- address envelopes

TASK 6
You are employed in the Travel Department of a large organisation in your own town/city, and this message has just been taken on the internal line.

> From the Sales Manager, Mr Robert Shaw
>
> Mr Shaw has to visit Newcastle-upon-Tyne next Tuesday and Wednesday. The Tuesday meeting starts at 3.00p.m. and he needs to know the time of a suitable train. He wants a seat reserved if possible. Also he requires overnight accommodation, preferably in the city centre. He says he is not quite sure what time he will get away on the Wednesday and will make his own return travel arrangements.

When you have all the information required, write a memo to Mr Shaw the Sales Manager.

TASK 7
You have an important appointment in two weeks' time which unfortunately cannot be made for the weekend. It will therefore be necessary for you to apply for a day's leave of absence.
Write a suitable memo to the Personnel Manager requesting a day's leave of absence and stating which day you require.

DATA PROCESSING

ELEMENT 3.1 *Produce alphanumerical information in typewritten form*

INTRODUCTION

What do you have to do?

▷ produce alphanumerical information in typewritten form

How well do you have to do it?

To achieve this you must be able to:

▷ produce 150 words or numeric equivalents in 10 minutes' working time with no more than two uncorrected spacing or typographical errors

▷ correct all errors neatly

▷ always keep information secure and/or confidential

▷ identify and report machine faults promptly

▷ always follow operating and safety procedures

What do you need to know?

▷ how to follow safety rules and diagnose faults

▷ how to care for and maintain machinery generally

▷ the layout of a QWERTY keyboard

▷ how each key functions and the use of fingering techniques

▷ how to position yourself for comfort and viewing

▷ how to make the necessary corrections so that they do not show

▷ how to use the printing facilities available

▷ how to use dictionaries/reference books/glossaries

What do you need to be able to do?

▷ prepare and set up the machine ready for use

▷ follow oral and written instructions

▷ produce letters, memos and envelopes

▷ plan layout of work

▷ key in text, proof-read and correct all errors

▷ store and/or produce a printed copy as appropriate

▷ report machine faults promptly

BACKGROUND KNOWLEDGE

Because the location of the keys is similar on all QWERTY keyboards – that is, keyboards whose upper alphabetic row of keys is QWERTYUIOP – keyboarding may be done on a manual/electric/electronic typewriter or a wordprocessor/computer. As with most machinery, once an operator has mastered the general techniques of one machine, the skills can be easily transferred to similar types of equipment.

Whichever machine is used, the operator must recognise the importance of producing accurate work, and this means that *all* documents must be carefully proof-read and *all* errors corrected satisfactorily. Always adopt the house style of the firm/organisation – for an example of a letter and memo layout, see Unit 2, Element 2.4 (pages 31–2).

It is advisable to have a dictionary available to check spellings unless, of course, the operator is using a wordprocessor/computer that has a 'spellcheck' facility. However, remember that even computerised spellchecks cannot tell the difference between 'their' and 'there' and 'where' and 'were'.

If you are using a **typewriter** you need to check that:

- the machine is at a convenient height and distance away from your body, is placed securely on the desk and is sited away from direct heat
- security precautions are taken and the typescript cannot be seen by others
- the paper is inserted correctly and is properly aligned
- the machine is covered when not in use to prevent dust entering it

If you are using a **wordprocessor/computer** you need to check that:

- the keyboard is suitably positioned for comfort
- the screen is ideally positioned for viewing in order to avoid body strain, and also to avoid eye strain caused by glare
- the screen is clean and the brightness is suitable for you
- the screen is sited so that it cannot be seen by others – for confidentiality
- the discs are always handled with care, kept in a protective cover when not in use and placed away from any source of heat
- there is a 'back-up' disc in case files are accidentally erased or lost, and all discs are stored in a lockable fireproof cabinet for security purposes
- the paper in the printer is inserted correctly and properly aligned, and the printer is on-line
- the printer is sited so that the printout cannot be seen by unauthorised persons

When using **any keyboarding equipment** you need to check that:

- your posture is correct. The chair should be adjusted for height so that your back is supported by the back of the chair. (Feet should be flat on the floor)
- the 'home' keys can be reached comfortably (arms and wrists level with the keyboard), and the fingers are placed correctly on the 'home' keys
- the layout required is observed; for example, line spacing, margins and (where possible) pitch
- the text is keyed in accurately, with particular attention paid to spelling
- good working habits are maintained, and the desk kept free from clutter
- the lighting, ventilation and heating are at optimum level
- the stock levels of stationery and consumables are adequate at all times
- all equipment is kept in good, clean, working order. Always follow the instructions in the operating manual and report faults immediately to the appropriate person

It is always advisable to have copies of all documents for record purposes.

THE TASKS

TASK 1 Type/key in the following recipe leaving a left-hand margin of at least 25 mm (1 inch).

SHORTBREAD] Centre
or
block

Ingredients

125 g (4 oz) Flour
 60 g (2 oz) Rice Flour or Ground Almonds
 60 g (2 oz) Castor Sugar
125 g (4 oz) Butter
½ teaspoon Vanilla or Almond Essence

Method

Sift all the dry ingredients into a basin and rub in the butter. Add the flavouring and then knead into one lump without using any liquid. Turn out on to a board sprinkled with rice flour and form into a smooth circle, 20 cm (8″) in diameter. If a shortbread mould is obtainable, shape the cake in that; if not, pinch round the edges with the fingers or mark it with a knife. Place the shortbread on a greased baking sheet and prick it all over with a fork. Bake in a preheated Mark 4 oven for 20—30 minutes, OR until the shortbread is golden brown and feels firm to the touch. Allow to cool before removing from the baking sheet.

Remember to proof-read your work carefully.

TASK 2 Type/key in the following letter leaving a left-hand margin of 25 mm (1 inch). Leave sufficient space for signature. Remember this document is confidential.

MOTORING ACCESSORIES]
74 Gilnow Park Road | Centre
WOLVERHAMPTON | or
WV2 5EJ] block

(insert today's date)

TO WHOM IT MAY CONCERN

Miss Mary Barlow of 40 Sycamore Lane, Wolverhampton WV5 3BH, has been employed by this company for 18 months. During this time she has carried out a variety of duties and has been assessed in some units of NVQ Business Administration — Level I, and has been successful in the following:

Unit 1 — Filing — Elements 1 and 2
Unit 5 — Stock Handling
Unit 6 — Mail Handling — Elements 1 and 2
Unit 9 — Health & Safety.

Mary has always shown enthusiasm and

> initiative in all the duties she has been asked to perform and is totally reliable. Had she not been leaving the area with her family she would shortly have been offered promotion.
>
> We are sorry to lose Mary's services but she leaves with our good wishes.

Remember to check your work thoroughly.

TASK 3

Type/key in the following advertisement, which needs to be sent to your local newspaper today. Find the address from the local telephone directory and address an envelope.

SALESPERSON VACANCY

Due to a reorganisation a vacancy has arisen in our office for a Sales Clerk. It is our intention to recruit a young person who would like to follow a sales career.

The actual training period will be 2 years and will include all aspects of sales work together with providing a good knowledge of our products.

Ideally the successful candidate should be aged 16—17 years, be enthusiastic and co-operative, have a pleasant disposition and be able to write legibly.

In return we offer a good salary, 5 weeks' holiday per year and excellent working conditions, including staff canteen and flexitime.

Please apply in writing enclosing a CV within the next 10 days to:

Ms Claire Foster
Personnel Assistant
Excel Supplies
89 Oxford Road West
MANCHESTER
M3 4EP

Check your work thoroughly.

TASK 4 Type/key in the following letter. It would be advisable to leave 6 spaces after the first dish and before the price and to set a tab. An envelope is also required.

JOLLY MILLER
81 Stoneybank Lane
MILTON KEYNES
MK6 4PU

Centre or block

(insert today's date)

Miss Judy Walker
Premier Training Centre
Northways
MILTON KEYNES
MK5 7JG

Dear Miss Walker

Further to your telephone call today we would be pleased to accommodate all your trainee colleagues on the last day of your course.

We have a variety of inexpensive bar snacks which are as follows:

Grilled Gammon and Pineapple   £4.50
Fillet of Plaice   £3.45
Individual Steak and Kidney Pie   £3.80
Roast Chicken   £3.95
All served with choice of veg. and creamed, jacket or chipped potatoes.

Pepper and Mushroom Pizza   £3.75
Quiche (with salad)   £3.20
Various salads available at   £2.95—£4.10

Sweets from the trolley if you so wish.

If you decide to reserve the room, please confirm your booking in writing and also state the time you will be arriving on Friday, 4 July.

Yours sincerely

Proof-read carefully.

TASK 5

Type/key in the following memo, which needs to be mailed to all branches today.

MEMO] Centre or block

To: All branches

From: Head Office

(insert today's date)

COACH HOLIDAYS 199—

Several printing errors have been noticed in our current Coach Holidays brochures. Please alter all your copies immediately according to the following amendments.

Page 30 Scottish Highlands. The price for a 7 day tour should be £268 not £257.

Page 34 Lake District. The departure date should be 8 June not 9 June.

Page 41 Eastbourne. The name of the hotel for all tours should be the Dorchester, which is situated on the Royal Parade, not the Cliffs, which is in the town centre.

Page 58 Isle of Wight. The half-day excursion to Ryde on the 6 day tour has been omitted. This is included in the price quoted of £249.

If you have already taken any bookings for these holidays please inform Head Office at once.

Proof-read your work carefully.

ELEMENT 3.2 *Identify and mark errors on scripted material, for correction*

INTRODUCTION

What do you have to do?

▷ identify and mark errors on scripted material, for correction

How well do you have to do it?

To achieve this you must be able to:

▷ identify all transcription errors

▷ check numerical data for accuracy, errors and omissions

▷ mark all data/text errors clearly for amendment

▷ conform to specific layout

▷ report and amend any uncertainty in text

What do you need to know?

▷ the method used for checking work from the draft to the final copy

▷ the relevant correction marks and their meanings

▷ appropriate ways of erasing and correction methods

▷ the layout and styles used by the organisation

▷ how to obtain information from reference books

What do you need to be able to do?

▷ use traditional techniques when checking printouts, typewritten and numerical material for errors

▷ identify and correct errors in spelling, punctuation, figures and layout

▷ make amendments in text/numerical data using appropriate correction marks

▷ use a calculator, a dictionary and other reference books

▷ keep to styles and layout used by the organisation

BACKGROUND KNOWLEDGE

It is very important that every business document should be checked for accuracy, whether it be a letter, memo, quotation, invoice or a simple notice for the staff noticeboard.

We are all aware of the saying 'Anyone can make a mistake', but in a business office we cannot afford to make too many. *All* work must be checked thoroughly so that errors, whether in spelling, punctuation or even layout, can be spotted and corrected before the document is presented for signature or before it leaves the office.

The need to check *all* figure work cannot be emphasised too strongly. Just imagine sending out an estimate/quotation and missing the last figure from it. This would be very embarrassing, and could be bad for the company's relations with the person receiving the estimate. The same error could happen in the Salaries section of a firm/organisation if the figures on the salary slip were keyed in incorrectly and left unchecked. You would be very distressed if the salary slip happened to be yours and the amount was lower than you anticipated.

Proof-reading is an extremely important skill. When we write or type something ourselves we all tend to read what we want to see, not what actually appears on the paper or on the screen. It is therefore necessary to train your eyes to spot errors and, with practice and perseverance, develop that skill until you can speed up the art of proof-reading.

When checking work that has been altered or amended, you must be able to spot the variations between the draft and the final copy. Always refer to a dictionary if in doubt about a spelling.

Sometimes checking may be done by two readers. If no one is available, a ruler might be useful to act as a guide from line to line. This is particularly good when used in figure work.

When amending material, printers' correction signs are used. The following ones will be required for the activities and the assignment.

Printers' correction signs (*continued over*)

Mark in the margin	Mark in the text		What needs to be done
l.c.	$\underline{E}$	underline the letter that needs to be altered	change to lower case
u.c.	$\underline{s}$	underline the letter that needs to be altered	change to upper case
NP or ||	$\lceil$	placed before first word of new paragraph	indicates new paragraph required
⟋	time⸱	letter(s) or word(s) crossed out	delete (leave out) as indicated
trs	⌐a⌐e⌐	means transpose	put in the order indicated
⌣	se⌒t	join letters or words	close up, do not leave a space

Mark in the margin	Mark in the text	What needs to be done
letter(s) required	⋏ where insertion required	insert what is indicated in margin
#	⋏ between letter or words	space required
⊙	⋏ at point to be inserted	insert full stop
⸴⋏	⋏ at point to be inserted	insert comma
/–/	⋏ at point to be inserted	insert hyphen
⅃	⊢——[	indent to be cancelled – block paragraph required
‖	‖ to be placed where margin is irregular	align print/type to correct margin setting

Printer's correction signs

Example

```
l.c  The Dictionary contains thousands of words and
,⋏   is available to tell you what a word means⋏ but
o⋏   it does not tell you which word to chose for
tr's your particular need. Here are some rules
NP   which might be useful to follow. [Pick out the
really⋏ shortest word that will⋏say what you mean. It
‖ ‖      is not necessary to use long words in a
⊙    business letter⋏

⅃ ⊢—[Be accurate by choosing the word which
⊂ express es exactly what you wish to convey.

u.c. the appropriate word in a business letter is
#    nearly always the shortest and simplest that
o/   will express your meanings.
```

Corrected version

The dictionary contains thousands of words and
is available to tell you what a word means, but
it does not tell you which word to choose for
your particular need. Here are some rules
which might be useful to follow.

Pick out the shortest word that will really
say what you mean. It is not necessary to
use long words in a business letter.

Be accurate by choosing the word which
expresses exactly what you wish to convey.

The appropriate word in a business letter is
nearly always the shortest and simplest that
will express your meaning.

THE TASKS

Resources required by students/trainees

You will each require photocopies of the following:

▷ Task 1 – the passage on computer furniture – one copy

▷ Task 2 – the keyed-in memo – one copy

▷ Task 3 – the printout/typed copy requested by MT – one copy

▷ Task 4 – the hard copy of an advertisement – one copy

▷ Task 5 – the rekeyed salaries sheet – one copy

▷ Task 6 – the retyped internal room/telephone list – one copy

▷ Task 8 – the twelve extracts – one copy

▷ Task 9 – the typed/keyed-in hotel advertisement – one copy

You will also require:

▷ Tasks 1–9 – a ruler and a dictionary

▷ Task 3 – a calculator

TASK 1 Read through the passage on computer furniture and make any necessary corrections.

TASK 2 Before the keyed-in memo is submitted to Mrs Cooper, the Personnel Manager, for her to initial, it needs to be proof-read. Check with the handwritten copy that follows, and identify and mark clearly any errors you may find on the keyed-in copy.

MEMO

To: All Employees
From: Personnel Manager
Ref: AG/ac
10 July 199–

FLEXITIME

It has been suggested that the introduction of Flexitime would be beneficial both to the firm and to many of the employees. Before making a definite decision I would like to have a meeting of ALL employees at the end of Friday's lunchbreak, i.e. 1.00pm. It is important that all employees attend this meeting which will provide an opportunity to discuss the advantages and disadvantages of such a scheme.

Please consider your views on the matter during the next few days bearing in mind that a vote will be taken at the end of the meeting.

TASK 3 The printout/typed copy requested by MT (Melanie Thorpe) needs checking from the original manuscript that follows. Mark any differences you may find on the printout/typed copy. Use a calculator to check the totals.

URGENT

I have requested this table to be keyed in on the wp or typed. When the final copy is received will you please check it for me as I will be away from the office for the next two days.

I didn't have time to check the totals — perhaps you would do this for me?

Thanks MT

376	069	514	621	193
829	704	360	492	534
240	933	171	133	317
797	819	236	915	806
357	668	101	143	627
654	468	758	125	390
416	345	603	301	751
125	720	512	364	488
502	475	266	304	919
294	104	080	227	636

TOTALS: 4590   5305   3601   3425   5661

TASK 4

Check the hard copy of an advertisement with the manuscript copy that follows. Use recognisable correction marks to indicate any errors which may have been made on the hard copy.

TEMPS   TEMPS   TEMPS

We have a good reputation in the area for supplying quality temporary full and part-time staff, and at the moment we have the following vacancies on our books:

SECRETARIES
SHORTHAND TYPISTS
AUDIO TYPISTS
CLERK TYPISTS
VDU/WP OPERATORS
COMPUTER OPERATORS
TELEPHONISTS
RECEPTIONISTS
WAGES/GENERAL CLERICAL ASSISTANTS

Why not call in and discuss the vacancy that interests you? Our staff are most helpful.

NEW HORIZONS
56 DEANSGATE
BLACKTOWN

OR

TELEPHONE (0936) 42756

TASK 5

Check the rekeyed salaries sheet with the list below, which has been amended to show the new salary pay awards. Mark any errors/differences you may find on the rekeyed copy.

Name	Employee no.	Date of birth	Present salary per annum
ALTON Mrs D	439	27.10.49	£13,450 £15,520
BAMFORD Mr J M	356	16.4.45	£17,400 £18,600
BRIDGES Mr A	443	10.12.54	£16,980 £17,958
COLEMAN Ms K	447	2.2.58	£12,800 £13,736
DAVENPORT Ms P	451	12.7.60	£11,950 £12,950
DEARDEN Mr F	364	28.1.47	£17,225 £18,100
HACKETT Mr M A	392	13.3.50	£16,445 £17,527
KIRKBRIGHT Mr O	463	28.11.58	£15,950 £16,900
MAYOR Mr R	477	3.1.60	£14,650 £15,560
PARKER Mr J E	468	19.4.59	£15,440 £16,400
PARKER Ms W L	479	21.6.62	£14,365 £15,225
PRESCOTT Miss W	482	6.5.63	£14,950 £15,842
REILLY Mr S P	473	15.9.61	£15,700 £16,660
RELPH Mrs B	491	17.10.64	£12,455 £13,395
SEDDON Mrs A	459	8.8.56	£16,258 £17,150
TALBOT Ms D	501	12.2.67	£11,432 £12,316
TATTERSALL Mr M J	426	14.11.48	£16,775 £17,700
WHALLEY Mr A R	495	15.3.65	£15,200 £16,175
WRIGHT Mrs T	499	19.5.66	£12,002 £13,050
YATES Mr D A	359	16.12.46	£17,846 £18,735

TASK 6

Carry out the instructions attached to the internal room/telephone list that follows, and mark any errors for correction on the retyped copy.

The internal room telephone list has just been retyped but needs to be checked from the original, which may be a little difficult to follow as alterations have had to be made when employees have left the company. Please make sure that all the surnames are in alphabetical order as well as the correct information in the right place. Should there be any errors please amend them and I will arrange for the list to be retyped or keyed in on the WP. It would be awful if a caller was sent to the wrong room or connected to the wrong telephone extension!

Name	Department	Room no.	Telephone extension no.
BAMFORD Mr J M	Accounts/Finance	12	201
BRIDGES Mr A	Transport	21	215
~~CHADWICK Mrs E F~~ *ALTON Mrs D*	Personnel	16	207
COLEMAN Ms K	Accounts/Finance	13	203
DEARDEN Mr F	Sales	18	210
~~GRUNDY Ms F~~ *DAVENPORT Ms P*	Advertising	15	206
~~GARDINER Mr D E~~ *(HAS NOW LEFT THE COMPANY)*	~~Accounts/Finance~~	~~12~~	~~202~~
HACKETT Mr M A	Sales	19	211
KIRKBRIGHT Mr O	Production	20	214
MAYOR Mr R	Production	20	213
~~NORRIS Mrs JJ~~ *SEDDON Mrs A*	Personnel	16	207
PARKER Mr J E	Sales	18	209
PARKER Ms W L	Personnel	17	208
PRESCOTT Miss W	Marketing/Research	14	204
REILLY Mr S P	Transport	22	216
RELPH Mrs B	Accounts/Finance	12	201
~~ROBINSON Mr B~~ *YATES Mr D A*	Personnel	16	207
TALBOT Ms D	Sales	18	210
TATTERSALL Mr M J	Accounts/Finance	12	201
WHALLEY Mr A R	Marketing/Research	14	205
WRIGHT Mrs T	Accounts/Finance	12	202

In the following twelve sentences, six of the underlined words are spelled correctly and six are not. List the numbers of the sentences that are correct. Give the correct spellings for those words spelt incorrectly.

1   As these purchases are for different people will you please issue <u>seperate</u> receipts for each item?

2   The <u>advertisement</u> in the local newspaper for a wordprocessor operator did not state what age the applicant should be.

3   This note is to remind you that the Social Committee meeting which was <u>cancelled</u> last week has now been rearranged for next Thursday at 2 p.m.

4   I am <u>dissatisfied</u> with the decorating which has been carried out at the village hall and I shall write a letter of complaint to the firm concerned.

5   It was <u>advisible</u> not to get involved in the political argument taking place at the club yesterday.

6   The lady you saw me with at the conference was an <u>aquaintance</u>, not a friend.

7   While having a driving lesson with a motoring instructor the learner accidentally put his foot on the <u>accelerator</u> instead of the brake.

8   I insisted that I be given an <u>itinerary</u> when I booked my holiday at the local travel agents.

9   The Health and Safety Officer said, 'Move that <u>parrafin</u> heater to the other side of the room; it will get knocked over where it is.'

10   Success is usually only <u>achieved</u> by great effort and sacrifice on the part of the learner.

11   When contemplating buying a <u>refridgerator</u> or freezer there are two things to consider. The first is whether the cubic capacity is suitable for the size of the family, bearing in mind its needs. The second is whether there is space available in the kitchen to accommodate it.

12   In order to keep a business running smoothly and <u>efficently</u> the recruitment of staff must be carefully planned. Once the applications are received a rigorous selection procedure begins and finally an appointment is made.

Indicate the errors in the twelve extracts by using recognisable correction marks.

TASK 9 An advertisement for the hotel you work in has been typed/keyed in ready for Thursday's and Friday's edition of selected newspapers. Check the advertisement with the original handwritten draft which follows, and indicate on the typed/keyed-in copy any corrections that need to be made, using recognisable correction marks.

We are opening our four-star hotel next Monday. The hotel is situated on the outskirts of the city on the Northern Road and is easily accessible by rail and road. There is ample free car parking supervised by an attendant.

The hotel accommodation is definitely superb with full central heating in all rooms. Three lifts service all floors. All bedrooms, which are beautifully furnished, have private bathroom, colour television, telephone, air-conditioning and coffee/tea making facilities. Amenities include a laundry and valeting service, beauty/hairdressing salon, sauna and solarium, games room, free in-house movies and dancing each evening. Cabarets and barbecues can be arranged. There is a choice of excellent restaurants and bars as well as attractive sun lounge and coffee shop.

We know you will enjoy your stay at the

Tygil Hotel
162/8 Northern Road
ABERTOWN
AB2 9JP   Tel: (0906) 59234

To avoid disappointment we advise you to make your reservation now!

INTRODUCTION

What do you have to do?

▷ access a computerised database and make changes to the records

How well do you have to do it?

To achieve this you must be able to:

▷ deal efficiently with incoming data

▷ correctly enter new data into an existing database

▷ correctly retrieve required information from the database

▷ operate the computer following all safety and security procedures

▷ take back-up copies of the database files onto disc and keep them secure

▷ recognise faults with the computer, software or database files and report them

What do you need to know?

▷ how to operate and care for computers and discs

▷ the nature of computer-based files (databases) and their division into records and fields

▷ the commands for listing the files on a disc and for copying files from one disc to another

▷ the commands for operating the database program

▷ the format of your organisation's data collection form

▷ organisational rules for naming files and for security of data, both on paper and on computer

What do you need to be able to do?

▷ check data collection forms

▷ load the database program and access the required database

▷ sort records in the database

▷ make changes to the records in the database

▷ check changes on screen and save the changes to disc

▷ add a new record to the database

▷ remove a record from the database

▷ plan and organise work within deadlines

▷ follow correct procedures for closing down the database

▷ make a back-up copy of the database file onto a floppy disc

▷ follow procedures to keep the database files and input forms secure

BACKGROUND KNOWLEDGE

Modern computers are very powerful machines, and can search for and sort information much faster than a person can.

Much of the information kept on computers is organised into **databases**, a set of related files of information. Each **file** consists of a collection of **records** of information, all with the same structure. Each record consists of items of information called **fields**. The fields often hold information in coded form (for example, M for male or F for female). This speeds up data entry and eliminates many errors.

To control the handling of a database, a computer program called a **database program** is used.

Your workplace/training centre will have computers (micros, minis or mainframe) running database programs on which important files of data are kept. The data kept on the computer is very important to the running of the organisation, and its collection and entering onto computer is a time-consuming and expensive process. The files of data are often named in accordance with company rules, which help to keep a track of what information is stored where.

Data is normally given to a computer operator on **data collection forms** which will have been designed in the company's own style. Every effort must be made to check that the data collected for entry is correct and that entries into the database are carefully carried out so that incorrect data does not get entered. Normally, groups of records are entered at the same time; these are called **batches**. Records may also need to be amended, or deleted if no longer required.

At regular intervals, the database must be copied onto another disc (**backed up**) in case the original copy becomes faulty in any way. Should this happen, the back-up copy can itself be copied onto the main computer system and work can continue. Usually, some of the new changes to the database will have been lost, so it is vital that paper records are not destroyed immediately, but are filed away so that data can be re-entered if necessary.

The main data files, back-up copies on disc and paper records all contain information that may be highly confidential. Keeping data secure is very important, and the following precautions should be taken:

- normally, computers should be locked when not in use, and entry to the database protected by passwords
- back-up copies on disc should be kept under lock and key, preferably in a fireproof safe
- paper records should be kept in a locked filing cabinet until it is safe to discard them – by shredding them if they are very confidential

Employees who have access to the database should be aware of the organisation's procedures for collecting, checking, entering and securing data. They will also need to be confident in the use of the computer, its database program, directory and copy demands, and to know when things are going wrong.

After each session on the computer, the program should normally be closed down correctly and a back-up copy of the database file taken. If more than two hours' work are done on the database in a day, backing up at the end of the day would be wise. Some databases do not need backing up quite so often as they are not changed very much.

Employees should be aware of the Data Protection Act, which controls the way in which organisations can store information about individuals on computer. The individuals concerned have a right, under the law, to ask to see their record, on payment of a fee. The procedures set down within an organisation for allowing such access must be understood and followed.

Computers sometimes fail to operate properly. For example, your computer may not start up in the morning, you may have a power failure in the middle of your work, or a disc you are using may become **corrupt**. In these cases, it is wise to speak to your supervisor or computer technician.

They can decide whether an engineer is needed. You should not continue to work on a computer which you suspect to be faulty – you may do more damage.

To ensure good operation, you should handle discs carefully, not touching the disc's surface or bending it, and store discs in their sleeves inside a box to keep dust away. They should not be kept near a radiator or other source of heat.

Your screen and keyboard should be cleaned with a proprietary cleaner at regular intervals.

THE TASKS

Resources required by students/trainees

You will each require photocopies of the following:

▷ Task 1 – the printout of the product listing; the printout of the customer listing; and the data collection forms – one copy of each

▷ Task 4 – the file logging sheet – one copy

▷ Task 5 – the data collection forms for 5(a) – one copy

You will also require:

▷ data files

▷ a formatted floppy disc

Soft Soap

Soft Soap is a small manufacturing company producing soaps, shampoos and conditioners for hairdressing salons, chemists and other retailers.

The company has a computer system on which there are two files – a file of all sales of their products, called the Sales file, and a file of customers, called the Customer file. Several of the tasks below relate to these two files, and some of the tasks will require you to work on the actual computer files which your tutor will have prepared.

TASK 1

You will need to collect the two batches of forms which are ready for computer entry and some printouts to check them against.

One set of forms is of sales transactions. These sales are often telephoned into the office by the customer and the sales clerk completes a sales transaction form. S/he looks up the customer reference and product number from the printouts.

The other set of forms gives details of new customers. These are received from your own accounts department, who will have done a credit check on them to ensure they are creditworthy.

For each customer, you need to:

● make up a new customer reference – this is just a three-character code based on their company name

● check the customer listing to make sure that the code you have chosen is not already used by anyone else.

Each record should be complete, and individual fields should be checked to see whether the entry is reasonable and valid (for example, that a product code on a form is actually a *real* product code shown on the product listing). Remove the records you are unsure about and circle the field(s) that are incomplete/obviously incorrect.

With each incorrect form, decide what action you feel is appropriate, and make a note on the bottom of each form accordingly.

TASK 2

Recently, you will have had the opportunity to work with database files on computer. When you use a directory command to list the names of the files, it is sometimes difficult to remember the content and layout of each file from just its name. Find out whether your organisation has rules for naming files and, if so, why these naming procedures were chosen.

TASK 3

Use your workplace/training centre's computer to make a list of files related to the database you are using (for example, Soft Soap's files). You may need to use a DIR command. You may list the files on screen and then copy them onto paper, or you can print the list on your printer.

TASK 4

For this task you will need a file logging sheet. Load your database program and use the sheet to record the name of one of the database files you work with, a list of the fields in it, a brief description of the content of each field and the coding used, if appropriate.

TASK 5

This task needs to be repeated on three occasions.

(a) You will need to collect the two batches of forms for entry onto the computer. Some are sales transactions, the others are customer amendments.

 Load your database program and make the additions/deletions and amendments to the Sales and Customer files. Record the dates and times of each session. You should aim to complete a batch in 30–40 minutes.

(b) Delete the record for Ellen's Salons. They have gone bankrupt.

TASK 6

(a) Produce a complete listing of one of your database files (for instance, the Customer file) as a printout.

(b) Produce a sorted listing of another file (for instance, the Sales file sorted by Product Code), as instructed by your supervisor.

TASK 7

Make back-up copies of the database files you used in Task 6 onto the floppy disc provided for the purpose by your supervisor. Put the disc away in the appropriate place as specified by your workplace/training centre's procedures. Delete your working files from your hard disc (or master floppy disc).

TASK 8

Your supervisor asks you to get some details about the Data Protection Act. Either wordprocess a letter to The Office of the Data Registrar, Springfield House, Water Lane, Wilmslow, Cheshire SK9 5AX, or ring 0625 535777 requesting a copy of *Guideline 1 – Introduction to the Act.*

UNIT 4

PROCESSING PETTY CASH AND INVOICES

ELEMENT 4.1 *Process petty cash transactions*

INTRODUCTION

What do you have to do?

▷ process petty cash transactions

How well do you have to do it?

To achieve this you must be able to:

▷ ensure that cash handling security and safety procedures are always followed

▷ ensure all transactions are accurate, recorded and supported by correctly authorised petty cash vouchers

▷ report all irregularities promptly to an appropriate authority

What do you need to know?

To achieve this you will need to know how to:

▷ complete simple forms/records

▷ use a calculator effectively

▷ communicate effectively

▷ operate a petty cash system including recording procedures and authorisations

What do you need to be able to do?

▷ process petty cash transactions for at least one month

▷ support these transactions with copies of records, vouchers and receipts

BACKGROUND KNOWLEDGE

Details of cash transactions are usually entered in the cash book (CB). However, small payments are generally not put through the main cash book. Instead the cashier will credit the cash book with a sum of money allocated to petty cash and enter the relevant cash book page number on the petty cash sheet (for example, 'CB6'). The petty cashier will debit this amount, called the **float** or **imprest**, in the petty cash book.

The imprest system is the most widely used. Under this, payments are entered on the credit side and the book is balanced at pre-determined intervals, such as every week or month. Payments from petty cash must always be supported by vouchers and/or receipts. The petty cash book is then taken to the cashier, who will reimburse the petty cashier with an amount equal to the value of the vouchers and/or receipts. This will restore the imprest to the original amount. For instance:

1 January	The cashier gives the petty cashier	£100.00
	The petty cashier pays out during January	£97.95
	Petty cash in hand	£2.05
	Cashier restores imprest by reimbursing the amount spent	£97.95
1 February	Petty cash in hand	£100.00

To allow easy checking, control and security petty cash vouchers will be numbered consecutively by the petty cashier and entered into the correct columns of the petty cash book.

The amount of cash in hand plus the total value of the vouchers should always equal the original float. To complete the double entry, the total of each expense column is debited to the relevant expense account in the general ledger.

Petty cash vouchers and receipts should be filed securely. The petty cash money should always be kept in a locked cash box and placed in a locked drawer, cabinet or safe to which only the person responsible has the key.

VAT is generally shown in a separate column on the petty cash sheet. This is to enable the VAT to be reclaimed.

The formula for calculating VAT is as follows:

$$\frac{110}{117.5} \times \text{total amount} = \text{net figure}$$

THE TASKS

Resources required by students/trainees

▷ Calculators
▷ Rulers

TASK 1

From the information provided opposite, answer the following questions:

(a) In double-entry book-keeping, where are the details of cash transactions recorded?

(b) Where in the cash book will the cashier record the money allocated to petty cash?

(c) What is another word for imprest?

(d) What is the purpose of analysis columns in a petty cash book?

(e) Why is VAT shown in a separate column?

(f) How does the imprest system operate?

(g) What should accompany an authorised petty cash voucher whenever possible?

(h) What should the amount of cash in hand plus the total value of vouchers equal?

(i) Where should the petty cashier keep the petty cash?

(j) When is a petty cash book, using the imprest system, balanced?

TASK 2

Jane Basnett, the Office Manager, asks her Office Junior, Peter Hall, to deliver an urgent document to a customer who lives 15 miles away. Peter is to go by bus and the fare will be £3.50. On his return Peter presents his bus ticket and a completed petty cash voucher to Jane, who will authorise the payment. Peter will collect and sign for his £3.50 from the Petty Cashier, Bill Jones. Bill will put the vouchers into the cash box (in lieu of cash), lock it and put it away securely. Later on he will enter the amount into the petty cash book in the travel column.

   Examine the petty cash voucher below and answer the questions given on it.

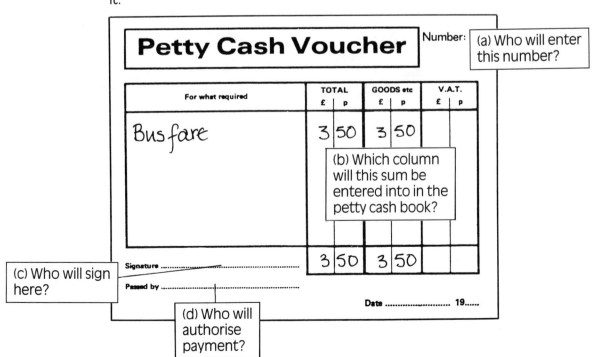

TASK 3

Examine the page of the petty cash book opposite and answer the following questions:

(a) What is the total imprest amount allowed for each month?

(b) How many petty cash vouchers were handed in for the month of January?

(c) What was the total amount spent on postage during January?

(d) How much cash was still available after the taxi fares were paid on 13 January?

(e) What is the meaning of the entry 'CB5'?

(f) How was the balance of £2.05 reached?

(g) Why is it important to number petty cash vouchers?

(h) What was the balance brought down at the end of January?

(i) How much cash was required from the cashier to restore the imprest on 2 January?

(j) How much cash was required from the cashier to restore the imprest on 2 February?

Page 12 of the petty cash book for Task 3

PETTY CASH BOOK

Page No .....12.......

Imprest £	Date	Details of expenditure	Voucher no.	Total £	Postage £	Travel £	Stationery £	Repairs £	Hospitality £	Sundry £	VAT £
15·00	199Ø Jan.1	Balance									
85·00	Jan.1	Cash	CB5								
	2	Stationery	1	5·75			4·89				0·86
	5	Postage	2	8·50	8·50						–
	7	Bus fares	3	3·50		3·50					–
	10	Staff association	4	9·78					9·78		–
	13	Taxi fares	5	6·00		6·00					–
	15	Gratuities	6	4·75						4·75	–
	20	Staff party	7	18·68					15·90		2·78
	25	Window cleaner	8	10·32						8·78	1·54
	29	Chair repair	9	29·37				25·00			4·37
	30	Postage	10	1·30	1·30						–
		Total spent in month		97·95	9·80	9·50	4·89	25·00	25·68	13·53	9·55
2·05		Balance in hand		2·05							
100·00				100·00							
97·95	199Ø Feb.1	Balance									
2·05	2	Cash									

INTRODUCTION

What do you have to do?

▷ identify discrepancies between orders/delivery notes and invoices

▷ identify errors on invoices

▷ report all discrepancies and errors promptly

▷ pass correct and authorised invoices for payment

▷ keep all records accurately, legibly and up to date

How well do you have to do it?

To achieve this you must be able to:

▷ check invoices against orders and/or delivery

▷ identify and report any discrepancies

▷ identify and report all errors on invoices

▷ pass correct and authorised invoices for payment

▷ keep all records up to date, legibly and accurately

What do you need to know?

▷ the purpose and use of invoices in business

▷ the functions of purchasing, sales and accounts departments

▷ the importance of confidentiality

▷ how to use a calculator effectively

▷ filing/recording systems

BACKGROUND KNOWLEDGE

Business generally exists to make a profit by either manufacturing, selling, advising or offering a service. In order to ensure the business operates efficiently, records of all transactions must be kept. The number and style of records will depend upon the size of the company. In a small company all the records will probably be kept by one person, but larger companies will have specialist departments dealing with each part of a transaction. The larger the company, the more departments it is likely to have. There are, however, departments common to all companies involved in offering goods/services for sale, which are of particular importance to this unit of work. The table below shows these departments and the parts of the transaction they are responsible for.

Purchasing	Sales	Accounts
Requisition	Catalogue	Cash paid out
	Price list	Cash received
Enquiry	Quotation	Petty cash
Order	Advice note	Company account
Delivery note	Accounts received	
Goods received		Accounts payable
	Invoice	Payroll
	Statement	Fixed assets
		Cost control
Payment		Credit control

Documents used in business transactions

The purchasing department of a company wishing to buy goods on credit will usually send an **enquiry** to a number of suppliers. In return they will receive catalogues, price lists and **quotations** from which to make their choice. The quotation will give the price of goods plus details of delivery and any trade or cash discounts offered.

Trade discount is a reduction on the stated price of an article. It is given to enable the buyer to make a profit if s/he resells the goods.

Cash discount is an allowance given to the buyer for payment within a fixed period. It is usually given to encourage prompt payment of bills.

On receiving a suitable quotation the purchasing department will place an **order** for goods. The order is usually written/typed on a standard form with a fixed number and sent out in numerical order. On receipt of the order the supplier will produce an **invoice**, which is in effect the bill for goods supplied and may be used in a court of law as evidence of a contract of sale of goods.

Invoices are generally multiple-copy documents produced on continuous stationery and carbonised paper. One copy will be sent to the purchaser as an **advice note** telling him/her the goods are on their way. Two copies will be sent with the goods as **delivery notes**. Both of these copies will be signed by the recipient, who will keep one copy. The other copy of the delivery note will be returned to the supplier as proof of delivery.

If the supplier makes an undercharge on the invoice, a **debit note** requesting extra payment is sent to the purchaser.

If the supplier overcharges on the invoice, or if goods are damaged and returned, a **credit note** will be sent to the purchaser.

The supplier will send **statements** to all purchasers, usually once a month, showing a record of all transactions in date order. The last item shows the amount due to the seller. When the statement is received the purchaser should check it against all invoices, credit/debit notes and payments made since the last statement. If it is correct, the purchaser should send payment, usually by cheque, to the supplier.

If the statement is not settled another copy will be sent. Each time a copy is sent a note will be made on it saying how many times payment has been requested, and the purchaser will be included in the aged debtor list.

THE TASKS

Answer the following questions. Check your answers by referring to the Background Knowledge section.

(a) List some interrelated functions of the following departments:

- Accounts
- Purchasing
- Sales

(b) Draw a diagram to illustrate the flow of documents between buyer and seller in a credit transaction.

(c) Which document is issued by the seller if there is an undercharge on the invoice?

(d) Which document is issued by the seller if there is an overcharge on the invoice?

(e) When and why would a seller give cash discount to a buyer?

(f) When and why would a seller give trade discount to a buyer?

(g) What is another name for an invoice?

(h) How many copies of a delivery note would accompany goods and what is their purpose?

You work in a small company and have been told that you are to be given a junior assistant to help with the processing of invoices.

Draw up a set of rules which the junior will be able to follow to assist in accurate processing.

ELEMENT 5.1 *Issue office materials on request and monitor stock levels*

INTRODUCTION

What do you have to do?

▷ issue office materials on request and monitor stock levels, using either manual or computerised stock records, and covering issue of stationery and small items of office equipment required within a department or small organisation

How well do you have to do it?

To achieve this you must be able to:

▷ use a calculator

▷ count quantities of goods in store and estimate requirements

▷ receive goods, check quality and identify discrepancies against orders

▷ store goods safely and correctly and check condition and quality

▷ issue goods promptly and keep and update records legibly and accurately

▷ rotate stock

▷ deal with damaged and out-of-date stock

▷ calculate usage rates and use reorder levels

▷ reorder following emergency procedures

▷ reconcile inventory and book inventory and report shortages immediately

What do you need to know?

▷ legislation relating to receipt of goods

▷ how to check deliveries against orders for quality and condition

▷ the procedure for storing and handling hazardous material and damaged stock

▷ how to issue goods and record as necessary

▷ standard and emergency procedures for reordering stock

▷ how to complete simple records and forms

▷ the procedure for rotating stock

▷ the procedure for storage, whereabouts and handling of goods

▷ how to deal with damaged and out-of-date stock to be written out of the system

What do you need to be able to do?

▷ make out and update stock record cards

▷ complete letters of enquiry

▷ order new stock if the balance is low

▷ deal with requisitions for stock

▷ find errors in stock records

▷ receive deliveries of stock

▷ tidy the stationery store

▷ do a stock check and complete an inventory reconciliation

BACKGROUND KNOWLEDGE

It is necessary to keep a careful record of stock held in a company/ organisation. This includes stationery for office use, which has to be controlled by an authorised clerk. This stationery consists of such items as typing paper, lined paper, memo forms, envelopes, carbon paper, brown paper, folders, labels, paper-clips, staplers and staples, sellotape, treasury tags, elastic bands, typing ribbons etc.

A careful record is kept of all stationery by using stock cards or by a computerised system. Under the stock card system, one card is made out for each item of stationery, with the name of the item written at the top. Under both systems, the records show the maximum and minimum stock levels for each item. These show the clerk when it is necessary to reorder the item. If too much stock is kept, money is tied up in stock and storage space wasted; but it is important not to run out of an item. In order to ensure that enough stock is kept, it is necessary to work out the minimum stock level for each item. This is done by calculating the average weekly consumption × (the delivery period + one week). The stock card or computer record shows the dates when the items were ordered and received, the invoice number and the supplier. It also shows the dates stock was issued to staff in the firm, their departments and the resulting balance in stock.

Ordering is usually carried out in a company by the Purchasing Department, and orders are made out to the various suppliers. Sometimes it is necessary to place an emergency order for an item which is required urgently. Different companies/organisations have different procedures for this. It is important that an emergency order is authorised by someone in authority in the Purchasing Department. If an emergency order is made by telephone it is usually necessary to quote an order number, and to follow this up with an official written order as soon as possible. Junior members of staff are usually discouraged from placing orders by telephone. It is important to monitor stock carefully and efficiently so that emergency orders are not usually necessary.

In some small organisations, stock is issued from a stock cupboard by a clerk or secretary. However, it is still important to keep accurate records when issuing stationery.

Companies usually have strict regulations on the issuing of orders and receipt of goods. Conditions of purchase are usually drawn up, and these may include the following:

An **official order** must be issued by the company/organisation for all goods supplied.

Acceptance of the order is considered to constitute acceptance of all conditions of sale.

If the seller wishes to increase the price, the right is reserved to **amend or cancel** the order.

An **advice note/delivery note**, giving full details and order number, should accompany each consignment. Goods received will be checked carefully against this advice note/delivery note. If items are damaged or quantities are not as stated, this note should not be signed and the goods should be returned to the seller.

A **statement of account** from the seller is sent to the Accounts Department of the buyer each month.

A **requisition form** is used to issue stock to staff. This shows the quantity and description of the goods issued and is signed and dated by a supervisor or other authorised person.

Stationery is usually issued at a certain time each week so that the stock clerk is not interrupted from other work. It is important to keep stationery stock in a locked store to avoid pilfering. The stock should be kept tidy and the shelves labelled.

Stocktaking is usually carried out every six months. The balance on the stock control cards or computer records is checked carefully against the stock on the shelf and any discrepancies are noted. If stock is missing, it may be necessary to check back the stationery issues for human error. If no errors can be found, the possibility of pilfering must be taken into account. Sometimes stock has to be written off because it has deteriorated in store or has become damaged.

When **receiving deliveries** into store it is very important to check the advice note/delivery note carefully against the order. This is to ensure that all the goods ordered are in the consignment, and are of an acceptable quality. If the delivery is satisfactory the advice note/delivery note can be signed by the receiver.

Careful **storing** is required for certain goods. Inflammable materials such as cleaning fluids should be kept in a sealed container away from heat and handled carefully, using a funnel when pouring them to avoid spillage. Sellotape and typing and printer ribbons can dry out quickly, so a limited stock should be kept in store in a cool place. Paper should be kept carefully in boxes in order to avoid damage to edges.

THE TASKS

Resources required by students/trainees

You will each require photocopies of the following:

▷ Task 1 – the stock record form, the order form and the stock requisition form – one copy of each

TASK 1

You work for Young Wares plc, 18 Green Street, Hertford, Herts SG13 8EF, tel. 0992 75361.

(a) Make out a stock record card for A4 white bond paper (stock no. 300). The supplier is W. Crest & Sons, 23 Stuart Street, Birmingham B20 3BT.

The maximum stock is 100 reams.

The minimum stock is 20 reams.

The reorder level is 30 reams.

The balance in stock is 22 reams.

(b) As the balance is near the minimum, order paper from the supplier to bring the balance to the maximum stock.
Complete the order – the order number is 568483 – and date it for today. The price of the paper is £1.88 per ream.
Fill in details of the order on the stock card.

(c) On 1 December, Jill Briggins of Sales asks for 2 reams.

On 2 December, Josephine Bates of Accounts asks for 3 reams.

On 3 December, Maria Darrio of Purchasing asks for 1 ream.

On 3 December, Anne Sparks of the Typing Pool wants 10 reams.

On 5 December, W. Crest & Sons deliver 78 reams of A4 bond paper, invoice no. B32785/90.
Complete the stock card and show the balance in stock.

(d) Make out the necessary requisitions for the above and number them 1–4. Ask your supervisor to sign them.

TASK 2

Twelve requisitions have been received for boxes of paper-clips. They have been entered on the following stock card.

Stock record card

Description   Paper-clips

Unit   Boxes

Maximum stock 100   Minimum stock 20

Stock no. 14

Size

Colour

Reorder level 40

Record of issues and receipts   Record of orders

Date	Quantity	Req. no. of issues	Dept of issue	Invoice no. of receipts	Balance in stock	Date	Quantity	Order no.	Supplier
199–						199–			
1.12					90	5.12	62	10062	W. Crest & Sons
2.12	6	1	Accounts		83				
3.12	4	2	Purchasing		79				
3.12	12	3	Production		67				
4.12	20	4	Sales		47				
5.12	12	10	Personnel		37				
6.12	2	6	Purchasing		35				
8.12	62			61284	97				
9.12	5	7	Accounts		92				
12.12	3	8	General Office		89				
14.12	12	9	Sales		77				
17.12	7	10	Personnel		70				
20.12	1	11	MD's secretary		69				
21.12	3	12	General Office		72				

The stock on the shelf does not agree with the balance in stock on the card.
Check the requisitions shown below, and find the errors on the stock card.

Stock requisition
To   Stationery
From Accounts

Quantity	Description
6 Boxes	Paper-clips

Signed   Sheila Orr   Date 2.12.9—

Stock requisition
To Stationery
From Personnel

Quantity	Description
12 boxes	Paper-clips

Signed Julia Richards Date 5.12.9—

Stock requisition
To Stationery
From Sales

Quantity	Description
12 boxes	Paper-clips

Signed Deborah Sands   Date 14.12.9—

Stock requisition
To Stationery
From Purchasing

Quantity	Description
4 boxes	Paper-clips

Signed Len Pound   Date 3.12.9—

Stock requisition
To Stationery
From Purchasing

Quantity	Description
2 boxes	Paper-clips

Signed Len Pound   Date 6.12.9—

Stock requisition
To   Stationery
From Personnel

Quantity	Description
7 boxes	Paper-clips

Signed Julia Richards Date 17.12.9—

Stock requisition
To   Stationery
From Production

Quantity	Description
10 boxes	Paper-clips

Signed Bev Ingham Date 3.12.9—

Stock requisition
To   Stationery
From Accounts

Quantity	Description
5 boxes	Paper-clips

Signed Sheila Orr   Date 9.12.9—

Stock requisition
To Stationery
From Managing Director

Quantity	Description
1 box	Paper-clips

Signed Peter Parke Date 20.12.9—

Stock requisition
To Stationery
From Sales

Quantity	Description
20 boxes	Paper-clips

Signed Deborah Sands Date 4.12.9—

Stock requisition
To Stationery
From General Office

Quantity	Description
3 boxes	paper-clips

Signed Kate Moss   Date 12.12.9—

Stock requisition
To Stationery
From General Office

Quantity	Description
3 boxes	paper-clips

Signed Kate Moss Date 21.12.9—

TASK 3

An easy way of working out the minimum stock level for an item is the average weekly consumption × (delivery period + one week). This ensures stock does not run out.

Work out the minimum levels for each of the following items:

Item	Weekly consumption	Delivery period
A4 bond	20 reams	2 weeks
C5 envelopes	5 packets	1 week
Paper-clips	6 boxes	6 weeks
Staples	2 boxes	3 weeks
Black pens	18	4 weeks

UNIT 6

MAIL HANDLING

ELEMENT 6.1 *Receive, sort and distribute incoming/ internal mail*

INTRODUCTION

What do you have to do?

▷ receive, sort and distribute incoming mail

▷ circulate internal mail, including routine and non-routine deliveries

▷ receive registered and recorded mail, confidential, private and urgent mail and damaged and suspicious items

How well do you have to do it?

To achieve this you must be able to:

▷ receive incoming and internal mail

▷ sort and open it, using letter-opening equipment

▷ check and collate contents of letters and packages, and attach enclosures

▷ report missing items

▷ date-stamp all mail

▷ distribute mail to relevant departments, using a circulation slip if necessary

▷ sign for registered and recorded mail

▷ check, record and total remittances, and follow security procedures

▷ deal appropriately with confidential, private or urgent mail

▷ recognise and deal with suspicious, damaged or dangerous mail

▷ complete simple forms and records

What do you need to know?

▷ use of appropriate mailroom equipment

▷ how to attach enclosures and identify missing items

▷ how to complete simple forms and records

▷ how to perform simple calculations on a calculator

▷ how to plan and organise work within deadlines

▷ the departmental structure of your company

▷ how to operate commonly used mailroom equipment safely

▷ the procedure for opening and distributing incoming and internal mail

▷ the procedure for dealing with specialised mail

▷ the different types of remittance

▷ the correct procedure for dealing with remittances

▷ security procedures for remittances

▷ the procedure for confidential, private and urgent mail

▷ the procedure for dealing with suspicious, damaged and dangerous mail

What do you need to be able to do?

▷ open incoming mail

▷ sign for specialised mail

▷ follow workplace/training centre procedures for confidential, private and urgent mail

▷ date-stamp and initial mail, if required at your workplace/training centre

▷ enter details in the post book

▷ check and calculate remittances, using a calculator if necessary

▷ enter remittances in the remittances book

▷ follow security procedures for cash and valuables

▷ pass remittances to the cashier

▷ distribute mail to appropriate departments

▷ use circulation slips if necessary

▷ deal with suspicious packages

▷ complete a personal log book of types of incoming mail handled

BACKGROUND KNOWLEDGE

Mail coming into a firm is very varied and includes letters, job applications, advertisements, quotations, orders, invoices and statements. Some items may be personal/confidential or urgent mail.

It is important to open the mail as soon as possible after it arrives and distribute it quickly to the appropriate departments. In a large company the mail room deals with this, but in a small company it may be done by a departmental clerk or secretary. Mail may be delivered by the postman to the mail room or the reception desk.

Before opening the mail, private and confidential envelopes should be separated from the others and put to one side unopened. Mail marked 'Urgent' should be dealt with first.

Envelopes should be opened by slitting one long edge with a knife or an electric letter opener. This allows the person opening them to check quickly that nothing has been left in the envelope.

Some firms like the documents to be date-stamped to show when they were received. Private and confidential letters should be date-stamped on the envelope.

In many firms enclosures such as cheques, postal orders and leaflets should be firmly attached to correspondence.

If a letter contains money, cheques or postal orders, the person opening the letter may be required to initial it at the bottom. Different procedures exist in different firms, but all money received should be taken to the cashier and recorded, usually by entering in the remittances book. It is important to follow security procedures with cash and valuables. If it is not possible to give these to the cashier immediately, they should be locked in a secure place, such as a safe, at all times.

Registered letters, recorded delivery post and some parcels will have to be signed for when delivered by the postman. There are also many private firms delivering mail, and parcels may have to be checked and signed for.

Incoming parcels should be checked carefully and if the contents are damaged or items missing, they should not be signed for. In most firms all incoming mail is entered in a post book, and remittances entered in a remittances book.

Internal mail is distributed within the company. If a firm has several branches, internal mail may be delivered between branches using an internal post bag and the firm's own transport. Some internal mail will need to be distributed within the local branch. The usual procedure is for the post messenger to distribute incoming mail to the various departments, and at the same time pick up internal mail for redistribution to other departments. Reusable internal mail envelopes are normally used for this purpose.

Opening of suspicious packages

If a suspicious letter or parcel arrives, do not attempt to open it or examine it. Check with the addressee and look for the sender's name on the back. Put it in a room, lock the door and keep the key. Call your tutor, who will contact the emergency services if necessary.

The mail room

The planning of the layout of the mail room is very important in a workplace/ training centre. It may be convenient to have incoming mail equipment such as letter-opening machines, mail racks and pigeon-holes on one side of the mail room, and outgoing mail equipment such as folding and inserting machines, addressing machines and franking machines on the other side of the mail room.

THE TASKS

Resources required by students/trainees

You will each require photocopies of the following:

▷ Task 1 – the page from the remittances book – one copy

▷ Task 2 – the circulation slip – one copy

▷ Task 4 – the diagram of pigeon-holes – one copy

▷ Task 5 – the page from the register – one copy

TASK 1

The following remittances have been received today. Enter them in the remittances book.

Remember remittances should be passed to the cashier immediately, or locked away securely.

A cheque was received from Wilkinson & Swift for £542.60.

£1.20 in the form of a postal order was received from Mrs W. Barnes.

Mr J. Goodwin sent in a cheque for £15.62.

A cheque for £136.40 arrived from P. Broad & Sons.

Ms R. Wilson sent £0.38 in the form of postage stamps.

A cheque for £40.21 was received from Mr L. Smith.

A registered letter arrived from Mrs B. Preston, which contained £82.35 in bank notes.

Barnes & Price plc sent in a cheque for £326.47.

TASK 2

Circulation slips are used in an organisation to pass on items of incoming post to various departments that may find them of interest. These items might be catalogues, brochures, reports, journals, magazines etc.

A brochure is received this morning in the post. Fill out the circulation slip so that the following personnel will see it:

B. Watson, Accounts Department

Ms J. Roberts, Buying Department

R. Singh, Sales Department

Mrs D. W. Capra, Personnel Department

TASK 3

(a) What sort of mail should not be opened?

(b) How are remittances dealt with in your workplace/training centre?

(c) What would you do in your workplace/training centre if a letter did not contain a postal order which was supposed to be enclosed?

(d) How is post distributed to the various departments in your workplace/training centre?

(e) What sort of post has to be signed for?

(f) Would you sign for a parcel if the contents were damaged?

TASK 4

Your company makes stereo units. You are working in the post room dealing with this morning's incoming mail. Mail is usually sorted into mail trays or pigeon-holes like those illustrated on the photocopy.

Which pigeon-holes would you put the following documents into? Write the number only for each document in the pigeon-hole that you think it should go into. The first one has been done for you.

1 Letter enquiring about job vacancies
2 Letter for the Sales Manager marked 'Personal'
3 Letter addressed to the Purchasing Manager
4 Letter complaining about faulty LED (light emitting diode) display on a stereo
5 Letter from a customer complimenting the company on speedy service
6 Quotation from a builder about a new extension to the factory
7 Order for compact disc player
8 Ten orders for personal stereos
9 Electricity account
10 Statement from supplier
11 Letter enquiring about new programmable compact disc players
12 Letter from the accountants, who are dealing with company income tax
13 Advice note
14 Three self-certification sickness certificates from staff who are away ill
15 Literature about photocopiers
16 Catalogues from a firm supplying electrical components
17 Invoice for raw materials purchased
18 Credit note
19 Letter from the company's solicitors concerning the sale of land near the firm
20 Demand for payment of business rate

TASK 5

You are opening the incoming post and you need to sort it into remittances and other mail. Other mail is to be circulated to the relevant departments.

Remittances need to be sorted into cheques, postal orders, postage stamps and cash.

You then have to sub-total each form of remittance (cheques, postal orders, postage stamps and cash), as these sub-totals need to be recorded in the finance register.

After this you need to total the value of all the remittances and record this value in the register.

Finally, pass both the register and the remittances to the cashier immediately.

The following table gives the details of the remittances received in this morning's post:

Cheques	Postal orders	Postage stamps	Cash
11.21	9.20	0.28	3.72
4.78	3.50	0.96	7.86
18.62	4.75		1.29
1.47	11.90		
6.14			
12.18			
3.24			

Find the sub-totals, total them as required and record these values on the photocopy of the register.

INTRODUCTION

What do you have to do?

▷ prepare outgoing/internal mail for the post

How well do you have to do it?

To achieve this you must be able to:

▷ seal mail in suitable envelopes

▷ select appropriate packets and wrapping materials

▷ sort and weigh envelopes and parcels using scales

▷ use reference books

▷ calculate postage using a calculator

▷ use imperial/metric weights and measures

▷ stamp or frank mail

▷ complete simple forms and records

▷ meet postal deadlines

▷ follow mail procedures for routine and urgent mail

▷ use Post Office guides and services

▷ use express delivery and collection service agencies

▷ follow security procedures

What do you need to know?

▷ the use of appropriate mail room equipment such as scales and franking machines

▷ the use of imperial/metric weights and measures

▷ how to complete simple forms and records

▷ how to perform simple calculations using a calculator

▷ how to plan and organise outgoing mail to meet deadlines

▷ how to use reference books to calculate postage

▷ the procedure for dealing with routine and urgent mail

▷ security procedures

▷ Post Office guides and services

▷ how to insert letters into appropriate envelopes

▷ how to wrap parcels securely

▷ how to use delivery services offered by British Rail and agencies

▷ how to contact agencies for express delivery of mail

What do you need to be able to do?

▷ collect outgoing mail from departments

▷ check documents for signature, enclosures and addressee

▷ seal documents in appropriate envelopes

▷ weigh letters and parcels and calculate postage

▷ sort mail into first class, second class and internal

▷ stamp or frank mail

▷ follow security procedures for stamps and money

▷ sort mail for collection to Post Office deadlines

▷ deliver registered and recorded delivery mail to the Post Office

▷ use the Datapost Post Office service

▷ use the British Rail Red Star parcel service

▷ use agencies for express delivery services

▷ complete mail records

▷ complete a personal log book of types of outgoing mail handled

BACKGROUND KNOWLEDGE

Afternoons are very busy in the mail room as most outgoing mail is collected in the late afternoon by the Post Office. Post is collected regularly through the day from the outgoing post trays in each department or taken down to the mail room by staff, to avoid a last-minute rush to meet the Post Office collection time. In a small company, mail may be prepared in the general office.

Some firms send post to the mail room already in envelopes marked first class, second class, airmail etc. In others the letters are accompanied by envelopes and the postal clerk is responsible for putting the letters into the envelopes. In the second case, it is necessary to make sure the letter is signed, the address is the same on the letter and envelope, and any enclosures are inserted.

Use a suitable size envelope and fold documents with as few creases as possible. Window envelopes are used for certain business documents, so that the address shows through and it is not necessary to type the envelopes.

Seal the envelope and weigh it on the letter scales. Affix stamps or put the letter through the franking machine, being careful to show the correct date and postage. Bulky or delicate items may be sent to the mail room with an addressed label, and these items have to be put into suitable envelopes – perhaps Jiffy or padded bags – and labels securely attached. If parcels need to be franked, a label can be addressed and put through the franking machine.

Parcels should be wrapped with care using boxes, packing material, strong paper, string, sellotape and labels. They should have the name of the sender on the back and inside the parcel. Fragile items should be marked 'FRAGILE – PLEASE HANDLE WITH CARE'.

In most companies, a franking machine is used. These can be bought or hired, but a licence is needed from the Post Office. The Post Office sets the meter and seals it to correspond with the money paid by the firm. Every time an envelope or label is franked the descending meter goes down to show how many units are left, and the ascending meter goes up to show the amount of postage used. Before the descending meter runs out the meter must be taken to the Post Office and more postage purchased. Alternatively, a remote resetting service by telephone can be used.

The Post Office Guide is useful for looking up details of postage regulations, how to wrap parcels and what is allowed to be sent abroad. Free inland and overseas postal leaflets are available from the Post Office, showing charges for different weights and types of post and parcel.

In some firms a postage book is used to record all outgoing mail. If stamps are used a record may be kept and stamps should be kept in a secure place. Electronic scales are usually used for weighing mail, and addressing machines and folding and inserting machines can be used for sending out large quantities of mail for advertising and mail shots.

Mail should be sorted into first and second class, parcel, specialised mail and internal.

Recorded delivery can be used for important business documents to ensure they do not get lost in the post.

Money and valuables should be sent by **registered post**. A receipt has to be obtained from the Post Office for these, and special envelopes are used for registered letters.

Datapost is a Post Office express service which gives guaranteed delivery in the UK by the next working day (this includes Saturdays, but not Sundays). A same-day service is also provided if required. With **Parcel Force Datapost**, there is no limit to the total weight of a multi-pack consignment, and individual items can weigh up to 30 kg. Charges are based on weight, as with other Post Office services. **International Datapost** deals with countries all over the world and charges are according to zones.

There is also a **Royal Mail express delivery** service for urgent mail. This is charged in addition to first class postage.

Swiftair is a worldwide express service for letters and printed papers. Swiftair mail should be kept separate and bear a Swiftair and an airmail label. Swiftair items should be handed over a Post Office counter or included separately in a firm's collection.

Red Star is a British Rail parcel service for the UK and also other countries. The service offered is station to station or door to door. For the station-to-station service, a train timetable is available. A customer can select the train from the timetable and take the parcel to the Red Star parcels point at the station 30 minutes before the train departure time. The parcel can be collected at the station it is going to 30 minutes after the train arrives.

When sending a parcel, the customer fills in a consignment note at the parcels point. The parcel must be marked with the name of the recipient (not the address), destination station and the sender's name, address and telephone number. Charges are based on the weight of the package irrespective of distance covered. There is also a door-to-door service. The customer telephones Red Star at any time of the day or night and the parcel is collected. The International Red Star Service uses high-speed trains and air services.

Numerous private agencies offer a **delivery and collection service**, and these are listed in the British Telecom Yellow Pages. These services are both national and international.

THE TASKS

Resources required by students/trainees

You will each require photocopies of the following:

▷ Task 5 – the Federal Express Form – one copy

You will also require:

▷ Task 1 – the Post Office leaflets 'UK Letter Rates: A Comprehensive Guide' and 'Royal Mail International Prices and Services'

▷ Task 2 – the Royal Mail leaflet 'Parcel Force: Customer Guide to Services and Prices'

▷ Task 3 – the current *Post Office Guide*

▷ Task 4 – the following:

a recorded delivery label	two envelopes
two certificate of posting forms	an airmail sticker
an advice of delivery form	a Swiftair label
a registered letter envelope	a Datapost form
a registered envelope form	

▷ Task 6 – the Post Office leaflet 'UK Letter Rates: A Comprehensive Guide'

TASK 1

Using the Post Office leaflets 'UK Letter Rates: A Comprehensive Guide' and 'Royal Mail International Prices and Services', make a list of the amount of the postage for each of today's outgoing letters.

Name and town of addressee	Weight	Type of post
J. Smith, Bolton	60 g	1st class
W. Wellington, London	200 g	2nd class
B. Leyton, Birmingham	250 g	1st class Recorded delivery
L. Jackson, Hertford	350 g	1st class
R. Lang plc, Liverpool	small (G) 156 × 95 mm	Registered letter
Ms J. Brown, Hull	100 g	1st class
Mrs G. Wilson, Taunton	450 g	2nd class
S. Cooke & Sons, Sydney	80 g	Airmail letter
P. Garcia, Malaga	20 g	1st class
J. Cunningham, Cairo	40 g	Airmail letter

TASK 2

Using the Royal Mail 'Parcel Force: Customer Guide to Services and Prices', work out the cost of the following parcels to be sent out this afternoon. Make a list of the amounts.

Name and town of addressee	Weight	Type of service
M. Smithson, Vienna	0.5 kg	Standard
W. Levingston, Sophia	1 kg	Standard
S. Long, Banjul, The Gambia	0.75 kg	Economy
H. Schmidt, Berlin	2 kg	Economy
B. West, Sydney	0.25 kg	Standard
W. Wong, Hong Kong	1.25 kg	Economy
E. Dent, Brussels	1.75 kg	Standard
P. Dupont, Monaco	0.25 kg	Standard
J. Paulo, Vatican City State	2.25 kg	Economy
V. Thierry, Paris	5 kg	Standard

TASK 3

Using the current *Post Office Guide*, available from any Post Office, answer the following questions about today's outgoing post.

(a) Can a parcel of shaving brushes be sent to Egypt?

(b) Do you have to pay customs duty on a parcel valued £5 to be sent to Jamaica?

(c) Can you send a case of whisky to a client in the United Arab Emirates?

(d) What is the limit of insurance for a parcel to the Balearic Islands?

(e) You have to send a parcel by Datapost International. What do you ask the telephone operator for in order to have it collected from your firm?

(f) Your representative wishes his post to be redirected to a post office in Birmingham. Is this possible? If so, what should be written in the address?

(g) A parcel is in the post room, addressed in pencil. Can this be sent registered post, or does it need amending?

(h) A book weighing 0.5 kg is to be sent to a blind client in Sussex. What postage rate is needed?

(i) Which companies in Essex and London will supply franking machines for your post room?

(j) You wish to use the Post Office facsimile service called Intelpost. Where would you take your document, and what notice would be displayed there?

TASK 4

Obtain and use the appropriate Post Office forms for the following:

(a) Complete a recorded delivery label for a contract to be sent to Jones Builders, 57 Bridge Road, Norwich, Norfolk NR1 1RE.

(b) Complete a certificate of posting for a parcel sent to Johnson & Brown plc, 2 West Street, Worthing, Sussex BN11 2DY.

(c) Complete an advice of delivery form for a letter addressed to B. Sampson, 1 Lovelace Lane, Edinburgh, Scotland EH11 4EF. This is being sent by recorded delivery, so please complete the label and include the number of the ADC form.

(d) Using the appropriate envelope, address a registered letter to Ms L. Iameo, 27 High Street, Preston, Lancs PR1 8HU.

(e) Address an envelope weighing under 10 g to W. Tinsell, 5/321 Western Avenue, Monterey, Sydney 2217, New South Wales, Australia. Send the envelope by airmail. Work out the correct postage and frank your envelope.

(f) Address a Swiftair letter for M. Domingo, Edificio Costablanca, Torrenueva, Motril 18720, Granada, Spain. Send the letter by Swiftair. Work out the correct postage and complete a certificate of posting form.

(g) You are sending a package by Datapost to Dowell and Neuberger & Co, 98 Seymour Place, Hoddesdon, Herts EN11 9NR. Complete the necessary Datapost form, obtainable from the Post Office.

TASK 5

You are sending a parcel by the Federal Express Delivery Service.
Using the following guidelines on Federal Express, complete the form to be attached to your parcel. You will need the following details:

- Your account no. is M 1231.
- The sender should be Young Wares plc, 18 Green Street, Hertford, Herts SG13 8EF. You need not give a reference number.
- The parcel is being delivered to Mr. A. Cunningham, Research Projects, Windrush Gardens, Whitehorse Way, Amersham, Bucks HP6 6HJ, tel. no. 0865 883214.
- It is a personal computer weighing 20 kg.
- It can be delivered any time in the next two working days.

Complete the details on the Consignment Note and attach to the first package in a consignment

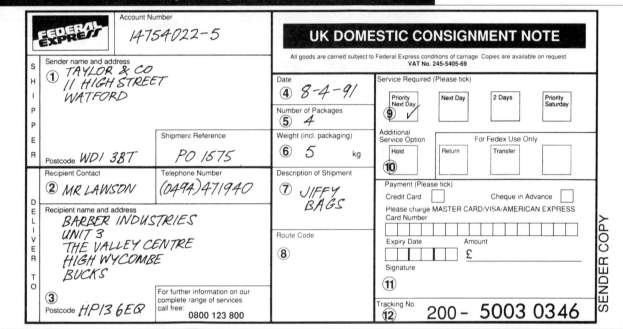

Step 1 Complete details

① Complete shipper details including your account number. Any shipment reference you may wish to use (eg Despatch Note Number) may be added. This will appear on our new invoice.

② The recipient details should always include a contact name and telephone number, to avoid difficulties at the point of delivery.

③ The recipient address MUST have a POSTCODE. Our new routing system is based around the principle of linking consignee postcodes to Federal Express' delivery stations at the point of collection. This provides accurate routing throughout transit. Therefore a correct postcode on every single package is imperative.

N.B. WE ARE UNABLE TO HONOUR OUR GUARANTEE IN THE ABSENCE OF A CORRECT POSTCODE.

④ Enter the date of despatch (when Federal Express collect your consignment).

⑤ Enter the number of packages in the shipment.

⑥ Weight, in kilograms, should include packaging.

⑦ The description can be particularly useful when shipping a number of different shaped items in one consignment – details that help us check packages in transit.

⑧ The route code should not be completed as this is applied by the courier during collection.

⑨ Tick the service required, remembering that only one box should be marked.

⑩ Tick the service option box, if relevant.

⑪ If you are not a Federal Express account holder you have the opportunity to pay by cheque or credit card.

⑫ To obtain shipment status and, perhaps more importantly, proof of delivery information, call free 0800 123 800 and quote the main consignment tracking number.

Step 2 Attach the note to the first package

Remove the adhesive backing, as marked, and attach the consignment note to the first package in a shipment ie, to a single-piece shipment, or the first package in a multi-piece shipment.

NB. THERE IS NO NEED TO ATTACH A SERVICE LABEL TO THIS FIRST PACKAGE

The courier will check the shipment details, apply a route code and scan the package barcode. Our courier will also remove the top copy of the consignment note, the SENDER COPY, which you can retain as a reference of your shipment.

TASK 6

The following is a list of this afternoon's outgoing post.

(a) Use the Post Office leaflet 'UK Letter Rates: A Comprehensive Guide' to make two lists: head one 'Weight of letters' and the other 'Cost of postage'.

Type of postage	Average weight per letter	No. of letters
2nd class	31 g	614
1st class	25 g	310
2nd class	120 g	51
1st class	142 g	46
2nd class	232 g	34
1st class	351 g	26
2nd class	414 g	17
1st class	512 g	8
2nd class	642 g	4
1st class	721 g	2
	Totals	

(b) Using the number of letters and the average weight per letter, find the total weight for each row across.

(c) Find the postage cost for each row by multiplying the number of letters in the row by the cost for one letter.

(d) Find the totals of the last column shown here, and of each of your two lists.

(e) One letter needs to be sent by recorded delivery, first class. The weight is 175 g. What is the cost of the postage and the fee for recorded delivery? What is the total cost?

UNIT 7

REPROGRAPHICS

ELEMENT 7.1   *Produce copies from original documents using reprographic equipment and materials*

INTRODUCTION

What do you have to do?

▷ produce copies from original documents using reprographic equipment and materials

How well do you have to do it?

To achieve this you must be able to:

▷ produce copies to specification and on time

▷ make economical use of materials

▷ keep records up to date, legibly and accurately

▷ report faults promptly

▷ arrange pages in correct sequence

▷ fasten pages neatly and securely using appropriate equipment

▷ distribute copies according to deadlines

▷ follow safety procedures at all times

What do you need to know?

To achieve this you will need to know how to:

▷ complete simple forms and records

▷ read and interpret instruction manuals

▷ operate essential equipment

▷ reject unsuitable quality documents

▷ recognise, diagnose and deal with equipment faults

▷ produce work to deadlines

▷ keep material wastage to a minimum

What do you need to be able to do?

▷ start up, operate and shut down equipment

▷ adjust machine controls for size, quality and quantity

▷ reject copies not meeting organisational standards

▷ make adjustments to correct minor malfunctions on machines

▷ maintain stocks of paper and printing medium

▷ carry out routine cleaning/maintenance procedures/safety checks

▷ report malfunctions/breakdowns

▷ sort, collate and straighten document pages

▷ staple/bind sets of documents

▷ operate collating and binding equipment

▷ complete records as required

▷ follow laid down safety procedure

BACKGROUND KNOWLEDGE

Photocopying is the most commonly used form of reproducing documents in an office today. It may not be the cheapest way, but it is quick, clean and generally needs no specialised skills.

There are many different types of photocopier on the market and the choice of model will depend upon a number of factors including cost, size, the number of copies required, the speed with which they are required and the functions which the machine can perform.

An office requiring little more than straightforward copying of black-and-white documents will choose a much cheaper and less sophisticated machine than the organisation requiring a variety of facilities. The larger photocopiers are capable of copying on both sides of the paper, collating and stapling. It is also possible to produce overhead transparencies, copy from books, reduce and enlarge text and copy in colour.

Photocopiers are generally easy to operate by simply pressing a few keys. Access can be restricted by requiring a code number to be keyed in. This number will register the copies made by individuals and is therefore a good way of controlling the use of the photocopier. If a fault occurs which cannot be cleared, it is important to know the telephone number of the service engineer.

Large organisations introducing photocopiers must decide whether to install basic models into all departments or choose a sophisticated model and centralise the facility. The quality and quantity of output from large photocopiers means that companies are now producing their own handbooks, advertising materials and brochures. The operator must be skilled in the use of guillotines, binders, laminators, joggers etc. Desk-top publishing on computers has improved the quality of the input to photocopiers and will probably lead to even more sophisticated machines, with skilled operators.

Machines may be either bought or leased and there are arguments in favour of both. With a leased photocopier a meter reading will be taken from the machine and sent to the machine supplier. This reading tells the suppliers how many copies have been taken during the last month, and they invoice the company for them. The reading must be taken on the date given by the supplier and entered on the meter reading card, and the card must be posted to the supplier. Toner, paper and other supplies may be ordered on the same card.

Although photocopiers are used extensively for copying business documents, some companies still retain the offset-litho machine for long runs of particular documents. The photocopier is gradually taking over from ink/spirit duplicators and it is becoming increasingly difficult to obtain spare parts for these machines.

Most companies will have details of the copyright law displayed by the photocopier giving information on which publications may be copied, how many copies may be taken and in what circumstances they may be used.

When operating a photocopier it is essential to ensure minimum wastage of materials and thus keep costs down. This can be done by ensuring that manufacturers' instructions are followed, the machine is kept in good repair and the correct paper and toner are used. Staples should always be removed before photocopying documents and paper-clips should not be put on the surface of the photocopier. If a large quantity of copies is required it is essential to take one copy first to check position, quality etc. before running off the larger number of copies. In this way wastage can be kept to a minimum.

THE TASKS

Resources required by students/trainees

You will each require photocopies of the following:

▷ Task 3 – the printing requisition form – one copy

▷ Task 4 – the stock record card and the purchase requisition – one copy of each

▷ Task 5 – the meter reading card – one copy

TASK 1 Ask for a demonstration of your company photocopier from an experienced operator. Take notes and, with the help of the instruction manual, prepare a checklist of instructions which you can follow in the future.

TASK 2 Find out how many pages of a 150-page book published in the UK you can legally photocopy.

TASK 3 Complete the printing requisition form for photocopying 20 copies, on A4 white paper, of a double-sided, confidential, 6-page personnel report. You require it to be backed, collated, stapled and returned in three days. Your department is Personnel, ext. 4139, and you are authorised to sign the requisition.

TASK 4 You have completed a large photocopying job and used 20 reams of A4 white bond. Complete the stock record card to reflect this on issue reference 1436. Then complete the internal purchase requisition to the purchasing department to bring the stock level up to maximum.

TASK 5 Complete the meter reading card for 25 April, showing 15000 copies on Model 907. Order five packs of toner on the same card. Supply the company name, contact and telephone number.

TASK 6 Look through office supplies magazines and manufacturers' brochures or visit local suppliers, and mount on A4 sheets of paper photographs or diagrams of a collator, a thermal binder, a spiral binder, a jogger, a laminator and a guillotine. Briefly explain how and when you would use each of them.

TASK 7 You have been asked to choose equipment for the quarterly company newsletter. This will have a circulation of 1000 copies of about 30 pages. List the merits of spiral binding and adhesive binding and compare the costs of each. Decide which equipment you would buy and state your reasons.

ELEMENT 8.1 *Receive and assist callers*

INTRODUCTION

What do you have to do?

▷ receive all visitors to your organisation

▷ find out their individual needs

▷ respond in the correct manner

▷ know when to ask for help from senior colleagues

How well do you have to do it?

To achieve this you must be able to:

▷ welcome visitors to your organisation in a businesslike manner

▷ find out what each visitor needs

▷ direct the visitor to the appropriate person

▷ keep the visitor informed of any delays which may occur

▷ keep confidential information to yourself

What do you need to know?

▷ how your organisation works

▷ where people are located and the layout of the building(s)

▷ how to deal with various types of caller – those with appointments and those without

▷ how to inform staff of a visitor's arrival – telephone, loudspeaker system, paging devices

▷ the importance of body language and what it means

▷ rules on security and confidentiality of information, and on security of buildings

▷ how to operate the in-house telephone system

▷ how to deal with difficult and aggressive visitors and who to ask for help

What do you need to be able to do?

▷ speak to visitors and different members of your organisation in the correct manner

▷ listen carefully to what is being said

▷ make appropriate responses

▷ use the right body language

▷ check the appointments diary

▷ record the arrival and departure of visitors

BACKGROUND KNOWLEDGE

All organisations have a structure. There is always someone in overall charge – the 'boss' – and there will be a number of senior staff with responsibilities for certain areas of work.

The receptionist needs to know where people's offices are and how to get to them, and what their internal telephone extension numbers are.

How to make this easy for yourself

Have a file which contains:

An organisation chart.

A floor plan of the building(s), showing where offices are to be found.

An up-to-date list of internal telephone extensions.

An index system of recording regular callers.

The receptionist is the first person a visitor sees – how you should behave:

Smile, look pleasant, and *mean* it!

Find out your visitor's name and use it.

Make your visitors feel welcome.

Pay attention to what is being said to you.

If someone has to wait, offer him/her a seat and magazines/newspapers.

Be polite, even with difficult people.

How you should look

Neat and tidy.

Clean and well groomed (hair, hands etc.).

Smartly dressed.

How to receive a visitor

Greet the visitor. Check the diary/appointments book to see if s/he is expected. Ask him/her to complete the visitor's book. Inform the member of staff whom the visitor has come to see that s/he has arrived.

If your visitor has to wait, explain the delay and apologise, ask him/her to take a seat, and offer magazines or newspapers. It is not often necessary for a receptionist to offer refreshments. Remember to be discreet and not to disclose any confidential information or to gossip.

Emergencies

If an accident should occur in the reception area, the receptionist needs to know basic first aid procedures. If necessary someone in authority should be notified and the emergency services called.

Body language

Do: smile.

turn towards the person to whom you are speaking.

look and be alert.

make and keep eye contact.

Don't: slouch or lean back in your chair.

frown.

look grumpy.

put up barriers – for instance, don't fold your arms or turn away.

THE TASKS

**Leisurewear Limited
– general
information about
the company**

Leisurewear Ltd was set up by the Managing Director, Mr Paul Peterson, in 1975 in response to the growing demand for leisure clothing.

Mr Peterson began the company in a small office with only one other person to assist him – Mr Clive Clark, now Financial Director.

Mr Peterson and Mr Clark are determined that the company should expand, and are continually looking for ways to increase business. Staff are encouraged to put ideas forward at any time.

Today, the company has a thriving manufacturing section, its own transport fleet, a modern showroom, and superb accommodation in the centre of Lichester.

All employees are offered a share of the profits after one year's employment, and are expected to show an interest in increasing productivity and in maintaining excellent standards.

Mr Peterson likes to get to know all employees, and operates a system of staff reviews every six months. Both he and Mrs Helen Clarke, the Personnel Director, take an interest in all staff progress and they offer, where possible, promotion from within the company.

The Sales Director, Mr Dennis Johnson, is an ex-athlete, and is very knowledgeable in the field of sportswear and leisurewear. Both he and the Showroom Manager, Mr George Baxter, travel frequently to Europe and the USA to find new lines. In the absence of Mr Johnson, Miss Tina Allen takes charge of the entire sales programme.

The Chief Buyer, Mrs Jan Ravelle, runs the Purchasing Department with a team of six staff. Mrs Ravelle joined the company in 1982 when she came to this country from France.

Mr Nilesh Patel, the Chief Accountant, offers support to Mr Clark, the Financial Director, and runs all the day-to-day accounting procedures in the company. He has two assistants.

The Production Department is run by Mr Fred Windsor, and the Transport Section by Mr Jim Ford. Mr Windsor is an electrical engineer and has responsibility for all the machines in the manufacturing area. Mr Ford is responsible for the fleet of two lorries and four vans, as well as the cars used by senior members of staff. He is also responsible for the despatch of goods. Mr Windsor is the current Safety Representative for the company.

All Directors have a seat on the Board. This organisation chart shows lines of communications between staff, and who reports to whom. The hierarchical level is not shown.

Organisation chart for Leisurewear Limited

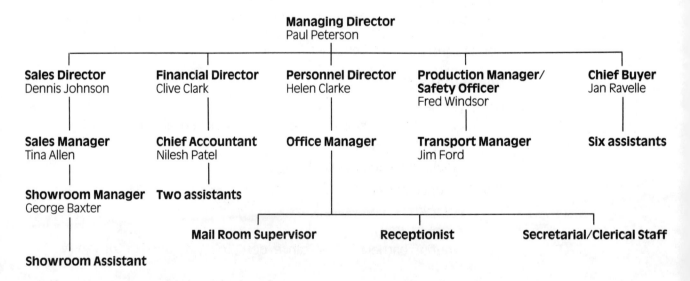

TASK 1
You notice this advertisement in your local newspaper. You think that you would be suitable for the post, and start planning your application.

LEISUREWEAR LIMITED
is looking for
a person to assist with
RECEPTION and
OTHER OFFICE DUTIES
We are a bright modern company in the
centre of town.
Salary £good! + LVs
Do you have good skills?
If you have, and are interested in sport and fashionwear,
contact:
Personnel Manager
Leisurewear Ltd
Lion House
LICHESTER
LI2 7PR
Telephone: 456784

(a) Make a list of the *qualities* which you think a receptionist should have.

(b) Apart from greeting visitors, what other tasks do you think a receptionist might have to perform?

(c) Now list the *knowledge and qualifications* which would help a receptionist in his/her work.

Congratulations! You have got the job at Leisurewear Limited, a company manufacturing and selling leisure clothing.

You have had a short training course to introduce you to the company, and to your job. You have been given the following to help you do your job effectively:

An organisation chart (see opposite).

A floor plan of the main office area (see next page).

TASK 2
Which of the following greetings would you use when a visitor arrives?

Leisurewear Limited, can I help you?

Good morning, may I help you?

Hi there, can I help?

Hallo, do you have an appointment?

Who do you want to see?

Yes?

TASK 3
Write out, type or wordprocess the following actions in the order in which they should be done:

Check the appointments diary.

Ask visitor to take a seat.

Direct visitor to correct office.

Greet visitor.

Telephone person visitor has come to see.

Ask visitor to fill in the visitors' book.

Inform visitor if there is a delay.

TASK 4

Using the plan shown below, how would you direct the following visitors to the appropriate offices?

(a) Mr Jamieson from Stretch Fabrics Limited. He has an appointment with the Chief Buyer.

(b) Ms Shah, who has an interview for a job.

(c) The service engineer to repair one of the machines on the production line.

(d) Three managers from retail stores to look at the current collection of leisurewear.

(e) The local fire officer to check all fire safety equipment and precautions.

(f) An important overseas customer with an appointment to see the Sales Director.

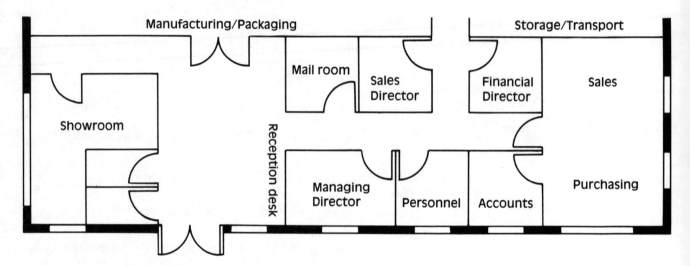

Floor plan of Leisurewear Limited

TASK 5

During the day, the following problems arise. How would you deal with them?

(a) You have previously been told that no sales representatives will be seen without an appointment. A pushy sales rep. who has no appointment arrives and insists on seeing someone in Purchasing.

(b) The Buyer from an important retail outlet arrives early for an appointment with the Showroom Manager. She would like to be seen immediately.

(c) A young man arrives twenty minutes late for his interview. He is nervous and obviously anxious.

(d) A parcel is delivered by a despatch rider. It is not addressed to anyone in particular, just to the company.

(e) An angry local resident arrives and complains loudly that one of Leisurewear's lorries is blocking his driveway.

(f) A member of staff returning from lunch on a wet day slips and falls, and appears to be quite badly hurt.

ELEMENT 8.2 *Maintain business relationships with other members of staff*

INTRODUCTION

What do you have to do?

▷ willingly respond to requests from colleagues

▷ be able to explain politely if you are unable to meet a request

▷ discuss openly any problems which may arise in the workplace

▷ refer any problems that you are unable to solve to the appropriate people

How well do you have to do it?

▷ use tact – remember you will enjoy your job more if you get on well with your colleagues, and this will require some give and take!

What do you need to know?

▷ how your organisation works

▷ what you are responsible for and to whom you are responsible

▷ acceptable behaviour and responses to senior colleagues – you wouldn't greet the Managing Director in quite the same way as you might greet your friend

▷ how to organise your time so that you meet deadlines

BACKGROUND KNOWLEDGE

Please note that as a junior employee you will be asked to undertake all sorts of different tasks. You should know your own job description and what is a reasonable request.

Examples of reasonable requests

purchase of small items for the office

assistance with cleaning of Reception Area in an emergency

staying late for something important

personal jobs for senior staff, such as booking a restaurant table

fitting in with a holiday rota

watering plants

making and serving light refreshments

Examples of unreasonable requests

large amounts of personal shopping for more senior colleagues

operating a piece of equipment without prior training

operating a piece of equipment which is dangerous

being asked to stay late for non-urgent work

having your holiday arrangements altered at short notice

You may wish to discuss these examples. Do you agree or disagree with the categories into which these examples have been put? See if you can think up some more for each category.

Working within deadlines
It is always important to meet deadlines. However, if there is not enough time to meet all the requests you will need to ask for help on what to do first – i.e., learn to **prioritise**.

Interpreting oral and written requests
Make sure you understand what you have been asked to do. **It is better to ask for help than to make a mistake**. But don't waste people's time because you didn't listen properly.

Getting on with people at work
In an office you will be part of a team, and so it is important to form good working relationships. These are based on respect for each other and a willingness to co-operate. If you respond willingly to requests and show yourself to be helpful, you will usually find your colleagues do the same.

Dealing with difficulties
If problems arise, try to discuss them calmly with the colleague concerned. If you feel there is a problem you cannot sort out by yourself, talk about it as soon as possible with your boss. If you have personal problems, seek help from the Personnel staff.

THE TASKS

An organisation chart and personnel details are given in Element 8.1.

The following situations could arise in your office. Study them carefully and then briefly explain what you would do.

TASK 1

You are working in the open-plan office of Purchasing and Sales. You have been asked to do the following:

(a) Jim Ford, the Transport Manager, needs you to check the database to find the taxation date for company cars and vans.

(b) The Showroom Manager requires a stencilled notice for the Showroom for tomorrow's catalogue launch.

(c) You have some typing work left from yesterday for Jan Ravelle, who is going on holiday tomorrow.

(d) You also have to sit on Reception during the receptionist's lunch hour.

In which order would you tackle these jobs, and why?

TASK 2

The weather has been very hot and you have been wearing brightly coloured summer clothing to work. An older colleague has made a number of personal remarks about your appearance and you are beginning to feel upset about this. How would you deal with this situation?

TASK 3

You have received a written request from Tina Allen to complete a piece of work to be faxed to her in Manchester this afternoon. You also have another important piece of work which you have already started, which is going to take all day to complete, and which has to be in the post tonight. What would you do?

TASK 4

You have been asked to assist the Sales Director's secretary in the preparation of details for a conference. The secretary has a day off to move house and has left you all the necessary information in the Conference File. However, as you start the work you find you do not have all the papers you require and you do not know where they are. What steps would you take to solve this problem?

TASK 5

Each month the Showroom hosts an open evening, which includes a buffet supper. The organisation of this is the responsibility of the Sales Director's secretary and initially she was involved in shopping for this function. However, for several months now you have been asked to go to the local supermarket alone and have struggled back to the office with heavy carrier bags. Today's list looks longer than usual and includes large bottles of mineral water. You don't think you will be able to manage this in one trip. You really feel this is an unreasonable request. Who would you talk to and what would you say?

You may prefer to role play this situation.

UNIT 9

ELEMENT 9.1 *Operate safely in the workplace*

INTRODUCTION

What do you have to do?

▷ operate safely in the workplace, including responding appropriately to common hazards to personal safety met in closed and open plan offices, in the operation of computer and mechanical equipment, and in fire and other emergency situations

How well do you have to do it?

To achieve this you must be able to:

▷ understand and act on instructions

▷ recognise and prevent hazards in the workplace

▷ follow company rules, safety policy and emergency procedures

▷ keep work areas safe and tidy

▷ respond effectively to an accident, fire or other emergency

▷ activate fire alarms, use fire exits and fire-fighting equipment in an emergency

▷ find first aid equipment, a qualified first aider and the accident register in an emergency

▷ safely move different items of office equipment

▷ care for and operate mechanical, electrical and computerised office equipment safely

▷ complete simple records and forms

What do you need to know?

▷ how to communicate effectively and interpret instructions

▷ the causes of accidents and hazards in the office

▷ the reasons for keeping the workplace tidy, safe and clean

▷ how to move materials, machinery and equipment safely

▷ how to operate and care for equipment safely

▷ the duties and responsibilities of employees under the Health and Safety at Work Act, 1974

▷ general procedures in case of accident, fire or other emergency

▷ when, how and where to get help if an accident occurs

▷ company rules, safety policy and emergency procedures

▷ the whereabouts of fire exits, alarms and fire-fighting equipment

▷ health and safety procedures in the closed, open plan and electronic office

▷ the whereabouts of first aid equipment and the accident register

▷ how to complete simple records and forms

HEALTH AND SAFETY

What do you need to be able to do?

▷ identify the whereabouts of alarms, safety representatives and first aiders, first aid and fire-fighting equipment

▷ complete accident forms

▷ complete the accident book

▷ identify and list hazards encountered at the workplace

▷ design a safety sign

▷ compile a memo

▷ complete a safety survey

▷ complete a questionnaire on health and safety in the electronic office

▷ design a staff handout on safety rules in the electronic office

BACKGROUND KNOWLEDGE

Accidents in the home and at work are increasing each year. The genuine accident is rare – most result from carelessness.

It will never be possible to eliminate accidents completely, but if everybody – whether s/he works in an office, shop, or factory – takes prevention seriously and is aware of possible hazards, it will help make workplaces safer.

The Health and Safety at Work Act lays responsibility on employees as well as employers, especially for safety and security. It is the duty of *everyone* to help prevent accidents in the workplace. Employees should co-operate with management in making an organisation's premises safe.

Care should be taken in the workplace to ensure that accidents do not occur – particularly with electricity, fire exits, adequate lighting, tidiness and equipment – in order to prevent injury. It is particularly important in a large open plan office where a number of people may be affected by safety hazards.

Electrical equipment should be switched off and unplugged at the end of the day, and faults repaired by an electrician. No-smoking rules must be observed, as smouldering cigarette ends are the main cause of fire. Employees should know the firm's fire drill and practice drills should be carried out regularly. Electric fires should be guarded, fire doors kept closed and fire exits kept clear.

Stairs and work areas should be adequately lit and torn floor covering repaired. Office doors and windows need to be locked at the end of the day to stop fires and deter burglars. Valuables, petty cash and confidential documents should be locked away.

In most workplaces technicians are available to move equipment, but if you have to move a typewriter, lift it from the back to prevent damage to the machine. If you have to lift heavy items from the floor, you should do so by bending your knees and rising with your back straight. Before moving any equipment or heavy object a senior member of staff should be consulted.

Health and safety is particularly important in the electronic office. If a new office is being planned, the installation of equipment needs to be properly planned. New sockets need to be provided and safe routes found for cables. Otherwise there may be a fire hazard and fuses may blow. Careful attention should be paid to lighting, temperature, humidity and ventilation. Computer print terminals can be noisy and may need to be kept away from other office areas. The workstations need to be properly arranged so staff can read the screens easily and also rest their eyes on the distance. Some staff may feel threatened by new technology and it is important to consult them in the planning stage. Adequate operator training should be given in order for users to become familiar with the machine and operating system.

Furniture should be well designed, and layout planned to prevent a feeling of isolation and boredom. Chairs should be adjustable and support the operator's back. Worktops should be big enough to accommodate all equipment and personal belongings.

Regular maintenance of equipment is necessary for safety reasons, and all equipment should be serviced regularly and repaired promptly.

There is some concern generally about eye-strain when using computers. Generally, opticians believe that it only aggravates conditions which already exist, and does not create a new one. However, all operators should be encouraged to have their eyes tested before using new equipment, and at regular intervals afterwards. Some experts believe that light green characters on a dark green background make the best combination for VDU screens.

No clear link has been established between radiation emissions from VDUs and harm to pregnant women. However, some staff may prefer not to use VDUs when pregnant, and perhaps ask for alternative duties.

Most managements negotiate with staff regarding regular breaks and rest periods. Short, frequent breaks appear to be more satisfactory than longer ones taken occasionally. Breaks should be taken away from the VDUs, and other tasks can be performed during this time. Breaks prevent stress and fatigue and produce greater efficiency.

Emergencies

In the case of fire or bomb threat, raise the alarm, evacuate the building immediately, and make sure that the emergency services are called.

Accidents

All employees should preferably have a knowledge of first aid. In any case there need to be trained first aiders in every workplace, and all personnel should know where to find qualified first aiders, nurses and safety officers. A first aid box should be available and its contents checked regularly.

It is important for every employee to know the company's procedure for accidents. Accidents should be reported as soon as possible, and entered in the accident book. This book should be in an accessible place, preferably near the first aid box. Particulars of the accident should be entered by the injured person or someone acting on his/her behalf. An accident form should also be filled in. Any hazards must be reported to the Safety Representative immediately so that steps can be taken to rectify them.

THE TASKS

Resources required by students/trainees

You will each require photocopies of the following:

▷ Task 2 – the page from the accident book – one copy

▷ Task 3 – the accident report form and the memo form – one copy of each

▷ Task 4 – the questionnaire on the video – one copy

You will also require:

▷ Task 3 – the page from the accident book for Task 2

Scenario

You are working at Young Wares plc, 18 Green Street, Hertford, Herts SG13 8EF.

TASK 1 How can we make places of work safer? List all the hazards in the office in the drawing, numbering them 1–20.

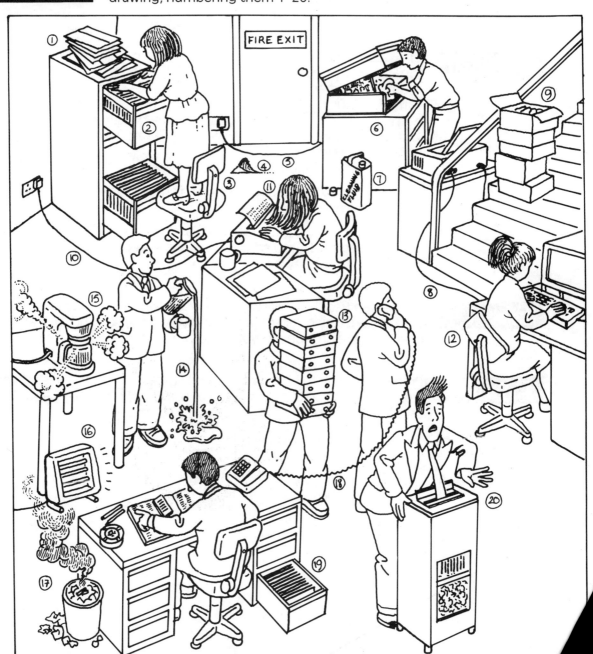

TASK 2

The following accidents have occurred recently at your company. Enter them on a page from the accident book.

(a) On 20 September at 1500 hours, Mrs Beryl Jones, a typist in the typing pool, spilt a pot of tea over her left hand, causing the hot liquid to scald her. She was treated by the first aider and sent to hospital.

(b) On 20 September at 1600 hours, Ms Joanne Preston, Purchasing Department, slipped on the wet floor in the typing pool, where the tea was spilt, and bruised her knee. She was sent home.

(c) On 22 September at 1200 hours, Mr Alan Simmonds, Sales Department, tripped over a trailing electrical wire and banged his head on the filing cabinet. He was sent to hospital for observation in case he was concussed.

(d) On 27 September at 1045 hours, Ms Joan Deakins, Accounts Department, received cuts to her legs when a filing cabinet overturned. The wounds were dressed and she was sent home.

(e) On 30 September at 0900 hours, Mr Martin Wilkins, caretaker, cut his right hand on some broken glass when emptying the rubbish bin. His wounds were dressed and he was sent to rest in the first aid room.

In your own words describe how all these accidents could have been prevented.

TASK 3

On 6 October at 1000 hours, Antonio Garcia, a candidate for a job, comes to the Reception area at your company, trips over a frayed edge of carpet and injures his right arm.

The firm's first aider, Ms June West, puts his arm in a sling and he is taken to hospital, where it is X-rayed and found to be fractured.

Mr Garcia's wife, Maria, is notified. Her address is 14 Weybridge Road, Hoddesdon, Herts EN11 8NR.

There is no damage to Mr Garcia's clothing.

(a) Fill out an accident report form and enter the details in the page from the accident book used in Task 2.

(b) Write a memo to the Health and Safety Officer from the Receptionist, reporting the frayed edge of carpet in Reception, and asking for action to be taken to rectify it.

TASK 4

If the video *Health and Safety in the Electronic Office* is available at your workplace/training centre, watch and study it closely and then answer the questionnaire provided by your tutor.

TASK 5

Prepare a notice, to be put on the wall next to the photocopier at your workplace/training centre, on how to use the photocopier safely. Obtain details from the photocopier operating instruction book.